DORSET

1   (overleaf) *Wool, the old Manor (Jacobean) and the River Frome. (This was the scene of the wedding night in Hardy's novel* Tess of the D'Urbervilles)

JOHN HYAMS

DORSET

B. T. BATSFORD LTD
LONDON

First published 1970

© John Hyams 1970

Text printed in Great Britain by Northumberland Press Ltd, Gateshead, Co. Durham. Plates printed and books bound by Richard Clay (The Chaucer Press) Ltd, Bungay, Suffolk, for the publishers B. T. Batsford Ltd, 4 Fitzhardinge Street, London W 1

7134 0066 8

CONTENTS

ILLUSTRATIONS

The illustrations are reproduced with thanks from the following sources: Kenneth Scowen—1, 2, 15, 18, 23; A. F. Kersting—3-9, 21, 25, 28, 29; Edwin Smith—10-12, 14, 16, 17, 19, 20, 22, 26, 27, 30, 32; Peter Baker—13, 24, 31

W I L T S H I R E

H A M P S H I R E

ourton
Silton
Milton on Stour
uckhorn Weston
Gillingham
Motcombe
gton gna
E.Stour
W.Stour
Stour Provost
SHAFTESBURY
Melbury Abbas
Fifehead Magdalen
Marnhull
Compton Abbas
Tollard Royal
CHASE
Woodyates
Pentridge
Sixpenny Handley
Bokerly Dyke
Hinton St. Mary
Sturminster Newton
Woodcutts
Farnham
Gussage St.Andrew
Cranborne
ehead eville
Hammoon
CRANBORNE
Iwerne Minster
Hambledon Hill
Shroton
Chettle
Wimborne St.Giles
Gussage St. Michael
Edmonsham
Shillingstone
Hod Hill
Iwerne Stepleton
Stourpaine
Tarrant Gunville
Gussage All Saints
Knowlton
Woodlands
Verwood
Ibberton
Durweston
Tarrant Hinton
Tarrant Monkton
More Crichel
Witchampton
Horton
Chalbury
Bulbarrow Hill
BLANDFORD FORUM
T.Rawston
T.Rushton
2
Hilton
Blandford St.Mary
Winterborne Houghton
Winterborne Stickland
T.Keyneston
T.Crawford
Holt
West Moors
ngham's elcombe
Milton Abbas
Charlton Marshall
Spettisbury
BADBURY RINGS
Cheselbourne
WIMBORNE MINSTER
Ferndown
Dewlish
Winterborne Whitechurch
W'borne Tomson
R.Stour
Sturminster Marshall
Milborne St.Andrew
olpuddle
W'borne Kingston
Corfe Mullen
Canford Magna
dle-wn
Affpuddle
Bere Regis
Lytchett Matravers
Turnerspuddle
Briantspuddle
POOLE
BOURNEMOUTH
Clouds Hill
R.Piddle
Poole Harbour
Brownsea I.
Moreton
Bovington
R.Frome
WAREHAM
Sandbanks
Shell Bay
rmwell
Wool
Stoborough
Arne
3
Blue Pool
ISLE OF
Studland
Old Harry
vermoigne
Creech Grange
Steeple
Corfe Castle
West Lulworth
East Lulworth
Kingston
PURBECK
White Nothe
tead Bay
Tyneham
Kimmeridge
SWANAGE
Peveril Point
Durlston Head
Lulworth Cove
Worbarrow Bay
Worth Matravers
St. Aldhelm's Head

E N G L I S H   *C H A N N E L*

CHAPTER ONE

Introduction

Like most of the English counties, Dorset is defined by largely arbitrary boundaries, except to seaward. Here and there a river divides it for a short distance from its neighbours—the Axe and the Yeo for a few miles from Somerset, the Moors River and Ashford Water for a little way from Hampshire, the Blackwater a mile or two from Devon. Bokerly Dyke serves for part of the north-eastern border, a reminder of the time when it was a fortified frontier. Otherwise you leave or enter Dorset at points established for administrative convenience or simply (and indefinitely) for historical reasons.

Oddly enough, both the eastern and western ends of the county boundary have in recent years caused discontent and dissension. In the west, Lyme Regis, lying on the edge of Devon, has hankered after inclusion in the larger county in order to share in the economic benefits of its reputation as a holiday area. In the east, Poole, having grown monstrous by Dorset standards, aspires to independence, which would have a catastrophic effect on Dorset's finances. At the same time, Poole itself merges imperceptibly with Bournemouth, with which and with Christchurch it forms a continuous urban area with a population of over a quarter of a million. The inevitable consequence is the suggestion that one authority should control all three towns, when not only would Dorset lose Poole, but Poole in the eyes of its prouder burgesses would lose its own traditions and identity. For the time being, however, Dorset's territory remains intact.

In its absent-minded way the landward boundary enwraps a

great variety of landscape and townscape. The suburban wastes of Poole form one extreme, the rolling chalk downland, which is half the county and more justly called typical than other scenery, another. Yet a further contrast is made by the stark brown and purple heath which Hardy used as a backdrop to *The Return of the Native*. Between the hills and the edge of the heath lie well-watered plains broken by hedgerows, trees, and parkland. Among the hills, comfortable villages shelter in quiet valleys where rivulets run placidly to fill some larger stream— Stour, Frome, or Piddle—a few miles off. There are thriving country towns growing a little too fast for comfort and too often littered with unimaginative post-war Council building. There are seaside resorts ranging from very small to pretty large.

The coast itself is a pageant of scenic tableaux. First, sand and mud flats by Poole Harbour. Then at Studland cliffs and pinnacles of chalk matching those of the Isle of Wight 15 miles to the east, and giving way to the yellow-grey limestone slabs of Purbeck. Chalk and limestone alternate from Worbarrow to White Nothe, ten miles of cliffs and coves and sea-sculptured rocks. Both this coastline and the sands of Weymouth Bay are dominated by the Isle of Portland, that grim, grey monster petrified in the act of rising from primeval depths. Trailing beyond it comes the long spit of pebbles called Chesil Bank, bare and inhospitable, and doubtless ghosted by the plunderers of wrecked ships and their crews. At Burton Bradstock and West Bay sandstone cliffs rear up, yielding to black clays with sandstone tops and culminating in Golden Cap, whence, westward, the procession trails (though not without upheaval) to the county boundary and the first glimpse of Devon at Lyme.

The geology of the county, from which of course the character of its scenery arises, has features of particular interest. Roughly speaking it falls into three parts. The chalk hills sweep into the county at Melbury Down, south-east of Shaftesbury, and roll across almost to the Devon border by an impressive chain of peaks, including Hambledon Hill, Bulbarrow, Nettlecombe Tout, and High Stoy. A southern range doubles back south-eastward from the country south-east of Beaminster to run parallel to the coast west of Weymouth. Reaching the sea at White Nothe, it forms the cliffs along the Channel shore for a few miles, interrupted in the Lulworth area. From Worbarrow Bay it swings inland again, making a spine for the Isle of Purbeck until the sea cuts it off at the end of Ballard Down, where the shining cliffs and the Old Harry Rocks mirror the Needles and their own parent cliffs of Freshwater Bay. The chalk lands have the look of similar country all over southern England—rounded, rolling hills, grass-clad and generally rather bare. Once Dorset sheep grazed them, but now the plough has largely displaced sheep where dairy herds have not. The fields are large, and littered with a hundred thousand flints. The settlements lie in river valleys, which cause them to grow in length, but not breadth, laterally confined as they are by the constricting hillsides. Yet it would be wrong to think that all Dorset's hills are chalk. The oolitic rocks of the coastal strip make an impressive range, and the Inferior Oolite, with other Jurassic formations, which extends from Weymouth to Burton Bradstock, then inland to Beaminster, the Melburys, Yetminster and the country west of Sherborne provides some of Dorset's most attractive scenery as well as here and there quarries of good building stone.

In the north and the west the Vales of Blackmore and Marshwood, the one overlooked by the heights of the chalk core, the other by hills of Jurassic rock, including Pilsdon Pen, the highest of all, are on clay with small, lush pastures, and a thriving dairy industry. In Blackmore, the villages have room to sprawl, and use it. Marshwood Vale was once famous for oaks, and is still pretty well wooded, but lacks any large settlements at all. Its roads are narrow and gorge-like, akin to those of Devon rather than the relatively broad ways of the chalk uplands.

Dorset's third part is heathland, a great expanse of Bagshot beds, largely clays and gravels, lying within the angle made by the two ranges of chalk hills. Geographically this heath—the Egdon Heath of Hardy—forms the western extremity of the Hampshire basin, in a triangle bounded by Dorchester, Cranborne, and Studland. It is split by the valleys of the Frome and Piddle which flow into Poole Harbour within half a mile of each other, while in the east the Stour, breaching the chalk hills northwest of Blandford, breaks it transversely, flowing out of the county near West Parley, to mingle with the Hampshire Avon in the waters of Christchurch Harbour.

Hardy's description of Egdon Heath applies no longer to what we now see. The sour soil which supported only heather and gorse has been bent to the demands of the Forestry Commission, who have established extensive plantations of conifers. Elsewhere the military authorities use great areas to train tank crews, and the heather and gorse are ground into the sandy podsol by their machines. Some patches remain intact near the shores of Poole Harbour, especially in the areas of Studland and Arne, but generally speaking the elemental heath of Diggory Venn and Eustacia Vye has vanished.

Even today, though, its population is slight, the human settlements in the great triangle lying, all of them, on the alluvial strips by the rivers. The exception is Poole, but Poole is so huge and out of character that in this context it does not count.

The geology of Dorset can scarcely be left without some note of the coastal strip. In conveniently ordered form this shows a splendid succession of Jurassic formations, some of which have been named after their Dorset locations—Portland stone and sand, and Purbeck beds, Kimmeridge clay and Bridport sands.

South of Poole Harbour a spit of sand is succeeded by a stretch of Eocene clays and sandstones, which give way to the chalk cliffs of eastern Purbeck. Swanage lies in a valley of Wealden clay, which stretches to Worbarrow Bay and is protected from erosion by a carapace of Purbeck and Portland stone forming the southern coastal hills of the Isle of Purbeck. These oolitic rocks rest on a bed of Kimmeridge clay, black, soft, and shaly, which appears at the foot of St. Alban's Head and forms the shore-line from Hounstout Cliff, west of Chapman's Pool, as far as Gad Cliff, near Tyneham. At Worbarrow Tout the oolites die out for the time, giving way for a short distance to Wealden beds, then to chalk. At Lulworth a remnant of the oolite formation remains, with scenically spectacular results, but otherwise the chalk cliffs continue to a few miles short of Weymouth. From Ringstead to the far west, the coastal strip is Jurassic again, though for 18 or so miles protected by the Chesil Beach. The Isle of Portland is virtually a solid piece of Purbeck and Portland stone resting on Kimmeridge clay. West of Weymouth, the geology becomes intricate, with clays and soft rocks occurring in disorder behind the shingle, and further west still, beyond Bridport, appearing in cliffs of grey and black, crowned in places (Thorncombe Beacon, Golden Cap, Stonebarrow, and Black Ven) with a layer of upper greensand that shines like gold in the sun. The softer black rocks give rise to frequent landslips, and yield an immense treasure of fossils.

The coast is the id of Dorset's psyche, and she hides almost all of it from industrialised and mechanised man by the simple expedient of not building roads along it or to it. Admittedly, this generalisation is as untrue as so many, and you can find places where you can not only drive your car but may even—for a fee—park it. At the professed seaside resorts, indeed, cars are reasonably well catered for. None the less, long stretches of the coast can be explored only on foot, and urban folk unused to moving more than a couple of hundred yards without mechanical aid are never able to enjoy some of the breath-taking views the walker sees.

It could perversely be argued that apart from the coastal strip the county lacks spectacular features of any kind. It has no craggy peaks and gushing torrents like Wales or the Scottish Highlands, no wild moorland to compare with Exmoor or Dartmoor. It has no Stonehenge or Avebury, no great cathedral (all its neighbours have—at Exeter, Wells, Salisbury, and Winchester), no enormous palaces like Blenheim or Hampton Court, not even extensive and unpleasant industry like the North and Midlands—and its major literary figure cannot measure up to Shakespeare.

Architecturally, indeed, its most exquisite treasures are of modest size, its greatest churches, Sherborne Abbey, Wimborne Minster, and Milton Abbey, splendid but less than overwhelming, its country houses (even Forde) distinguished and intensely interesting, but unmistakably domestic. Its natural features, too, by the standards of the sensation seeker are undeniably minuscule. Its loftiest hill is a quarter of the height of Ben Nevis, the longest of the rivers that penetrate its downs only 65 miles from source to sea.

But this a county of paradox. Huge earthworks cap the hilltops by small villages. The chalk escarpments often drop so abruptly that the hills (for instance, at Corfe Castle and Shaftesbury) seem as high as mountains rising directly out of the plain, which lies spread beneath them with every detail on a clear day picked out in miniature like the landscape surrounding Brueghel's Tower of Babel. Downland indeed has its own grandeur, and Dorset's monuments can offer stimulus enough to the imagination.

I once heard a woman remark to a companion at Maiden Castle that there was not much to see there. As she spoke she stood on a 60-foot rampart raised entirely by the labour of a primitive people working with their hands and clumsy tools of iron or bone —on one such rampart of three, and in places more, the outermost describing an oval 1000 yards along its longer axis and two miles round. About her was the tangible result of careful military thinking and elaborate administration among her barbarian forbears, beneath her the debris of two thousand years of unwritten history that ended only with the Roman conquest, when our recorded history began. The sweat and toil and planning, the agony and bloodshed! For her, though, there was not much to see, and one can only imagine that her holidays might be better enjoyed in the Dorchester Hotel than in Dorchester.

For Maiden Castle is only one (though the largest) of the hill forts on the Dorset downs, some vast enclosures, some smaller, many of them yielding on excavation finds as old as neolithic times. Along the ridgeways and on the heathland lie dozens of round barrows, marked on the Ordnance map as 'tumuli', while doubtless many more, especially in the fertile valleys, have succumbed to the plough through the centuries. Long barrows also appear, with a handful or two of minor megaliths, henges, and other remnants of early settlement, for people walked these hill-crests before Stonehenge and Avebury were begun. The Romans of course imprinted their civilisation on Dorset, and not only was Dorchester an apparently important provincial centre, with walls and amphitheatre (a converted henge), but a web of roads radiated from it and from Badbury Rings, showing the county's importance in the colonisation of the south-west. Roman roads, Roman villas, or at least their foundations, Roman forts, and the detritus of Roman life now in various museums, are part of the fabric of Dorset archaeology, and the great monument of the period is the Giant at Cerne.

After the ebb of Roman power Dorset lies for the most part aside from the mainstream of English history. Saxon and Norman were undoubtedly here, and now and again some great matter of state flares up to cast a bright glare into this rather remote corner of the realm. The Danes sacked Wareham, a Danish fleet was wrecked on the rocky shore by Swanage, and King Edward the Martyr was murdered at Corfe. These are perhaps the major incidents before the Monmouth Rebellion. There was some toing and froing in the twelfth-century Barons' Wars, and in the reign of Henry IV the Poole buccaneer, Harry Paye, scourged the French in the Channel and the Bay of Biscay in the name of the king and doubtless to his own profit. Noisy manoeuvres in the Civil War included an unsuccessful siege of Corfe Castle by a Parliamentary force and its final capture by treachery, but no one can claim that Dorset's part in the war was decisive. Monmouth's Rebellion was another matter. The Duke landed at Lyme Regis, raised his standard there, and was beaten away from Bridport.

Introduction

After Sedgemoor, as everyone knows, Judge Jeffreys descended on Dorchester to wreak the King's vengeance. The last event inside the county of great significance outside it was the episode of the Tolpuddle Martyrs, whose sufferings for the right of labourers to combine in defence of their interests holds an honoured place in the early history of British trade unions.

I do not belittle Dorset history. It has as much interest and character as that of other counties, but most of it lies along the byways of social and political change. Dorset in fact has tended to enjoy and suffer the consequences of events elsewhere, which its history therefore merely illustrates. Clearly this peripheral quality is not unconnected with the comfortable smallness of its towns and architecture. Great cities, great fortresses, great factories and ports and prosperity on the one hand, and great wars and tumults on the other, often enough coincide in time and place, and where the towns and fortresses are modest the events within and around them are less likely to be remembered and recorded. If it is true, as George Eliot thought, that the happiest nations have no history, the people of Dorset have for centuries been closer to contentment than many of their compatriots.

Change and the mid-twentieth century, however, are not leaving Dorset untouched. No one would wish—it would be quite absurd—to preserve the county as a huge museum. Its landscape and its life have grown and developed naturally from the technology of the farming, quarrying, and manufactures carried on in them, and as the technology changes so must society and its environment. This kind of evolution will continue. Poole, they say, will have half as many citizens again by the turn of the century, and the noise of the arriving newcomers will echo in the council chambers of Wimborne and Wareham. Road traffic in eastern Dorset will increase, and the beaches and open spaces, and even the waters of Poole Harbour, will be more crowded than today. Probably Dorchester and Weymouth will grow, and

North Dorset has already had a narrow escape from development at Gillingham, to house some of the people London has to spare. Again, changes in farming methods may produce more transformations in the details of the landscape.

All this upheaval results from policies and pressures originating a long way from county and town hall, and the need to cope with it is part of the price we pay for a rising standard of life among the great majority of our people. One can only hope that in Dorset at least the consequences of material improvement in the lives of large numbers of individuals will not include, like elsewhere, the ruin of the countryside and the further degeneration of the towns. They need not. The inevitable new road-building can be made tolerable by sensitive landscaping, the inevitable factory- and house-building by imaginative architecture and estate-planning. At present in so many Dorset towns and villages we can positively and literally enjoy most of what the past has left us. Medieval churches, homes of Tudor, Stuart, and Hanoverian nobility and squirearchy, here a Georgian street, there superbly laid-out parkland, and often selfless tree planting only for the delight of posterity—all this we now have. Unfortunately what the last hundred years has built must be classed mainly as aesthetic lumber, which one cannot easily imagine arousing admiration in 200 years' time. There are exceptions, and they will be gladly pointed out in the chapters that follow, but the general standard so far in Dorset offers little hope for the future. Of course, it is easy to be pessimistic, and at all times and periods enthusiasts for the past have often been unduly gloomy about the present. The best of twentieth-century architecture and town planning is very good indeed. But will the best appear in Dorset?

Above all, the coast must be preserved. Enlightened landowners have determinedly protected much of it from the developer, though many caravan sites could be improved with judicious screening, and the provision of car parks too near the sea by some remote cove or cliffscape can only lead to deterioration. In general, however, the coast is largely intact and should stay as it is.

To the first proposition in the last sentence there is one important and glaring qualification to make. During the last war the War Department took over an enormous expanse of heath and coast for training purposes. An assurance was given that the land occupied and the villages emptied would be returned once the war was over, but that promise has only partly been kept. Eastern Purbeck beyond the Creech estate, and including the village of Tyneham and Worbarrow Bay, is still in use for training soldiers. It is hard to believe that people's homes and so splendid a landscape are really needed for shooting at. Yet, in effect, that is what they are used for.

CHAPTER TWO

Poole Harbour to Bokerly Dyke

Straddling the boundary with Hampshire where it meets the coast lies the urban complex of Poole-Bournemouth-Christchurch. Because so many scores of thousands of holiday makers visit these three towns every year, and because their resident populations are constantly swelling, a high proportion of people not native to Dorset but acquainted with her, encounter her first at the imperceptible boundary of Bournemouth and Poole, perhaps at County Gates, or further south among the suburban pines of Branksome Park. Here the rhododendron-and-pine bordered roads, the lush and comfortable houses (late nineteenth and twentieth century, all of them), spacious private gardens with obedient lawns, the winding paths to the sea, carpeted with pine-needles and heavy scented in the mild and humid air, where elderly retired folk exercise their dogs in the even now Edwardian limbo of summer afternoons, all correspond to the popular (and inaccurate) idea of Bournemouth. Indeed Branksome Park and its neighbour suburb, Canford Cliffs, are the justification and origin of the jibe that the best parts of Bournemouth are in Poole, for until a very few years ago, the postal address of both areas was Bournemouth. When the Post Office decided it should become more accurate the misguided inhabitants raised a most discreditable protest, but it is pleasant to report that to outward appearance, at least, they have overcome the shame they felt at their association with the older but smaller town.

For Poole's history is far from respectable. Pirates, smugglers, and rebels burst into scene after scene. Corruption seeps from its archives like a fog rolling off the sea on a quiet evening. According to John Hutchins, the historian of Dorset, its reputation, or, rather, that of its people, was such that this couplet was written and gained currency:

If Poole was a fish poole, and the men of Poole fish,
There'd be a poole for the devil and fish for his dish.

It is fair to point out that Canford Cliffs and Branksome Park have their share in some of the lawless episodes in the story of Poole. The heath on which these suburbs are built is fissured by long, deep chines leading down to gaps in the sandstone cliffs that border Poole Bay. In the nineteenth century their banks and the land round about were planted extensively with pine trees, but even before that, when the heather and gorse which still erupt in purple and yellow patches in summer had the run of the sandy soil, they made excellently concealed routes to the interior for contraband.

But Poole's history is bound up less with its eastern suburbs, which have grown up in the last hundred years, than with the Harbour on which it stands and to which it gives its name. This great stretch of water, (about 10,000 acres of it), the largest natural harbour in the world excepting that of Sydney, is almost enclosed by land. The gentle curve of the coast at Canford Cliffs is continued along the south-eastern shore of the Sandbanks peninsula to its tip. Here is the mouth of the Harbour, a mere 400 yards of sea from South Haven Point, which is geographically part of the Isle of Purbeck. Within this narrow opening, through which the tide ebbs and flows with great force, lies a coastline almost a hundred miles long, deeply indented with inlets and bays, its shore varying from mud flats swamped at high tide to sandy beaches fit for sun-bathing. The Sandbanks peninsula itself, narrow and slender-necked, has been extensively built over, but some of the dunes from which it derived its name are still there. On the seaward side it boasts a wide, flat belt of sand with good bathing which gives it enormous popularity in the summer. Consequently the only road in or out is impassable on fine Sun-

2 *The Georgian Custom House at Poole*

day mornings. Facing the Harbour its shore is a muddy expanse overgrown with rice grass.

The north-eastern edge of the Harbour is entirely built-up, though an exiguous patch of grass and gorse remains, preserved as a view-point at Evening Hill. The west is mud, the south, mud with occasional beaches, and gradually the mud is taking over, the harbour silting up. It has been doing so for hundreds of years. A channel for ships is kept open to Poole Quay, an active and busy port, though relatively less important than at the height of its prosperity in the eighteenth century. A holiday camp thrives to the west of the town, and there is much talk of a yachting marina. Indeed, the Harbour's prime importance today lies in its use as an anchorage for an annually growing horde of yachts, and a vast sheltered lake on which to sail them. On a fine evening in the summer, the water at high tide concealing the brown mud of the flats and lying still as glass under a darkening sky, the yachts in scores and hundreds seen from the low eminence of Evening Hill sit on its gleaming surface like flies. When the sun is high, especially at week-ends, the white sails appear as gigantic foam flecks, persistent in some mysterious way, and gliding inscrutably about the extensive navigable channels of this wide basin of land-locked brine. Fortunately (for the Harbour looks its best at high tide) it is curiously blessed with, not two, but four tides each day, a phenomenon which occurs along the entire coast between Weymouth and Southampton.

At its old heart, on the quay and in the immediate vicinity of the parish church, Poole preserves something of the eighteenth century. Its discreetly elegant customs house, a handsome brick building with the look of a gentleman's residence, dates from 1813, when a predecessor on the same site was burnt down. The earlier building was the scene in 1747 of one of the more disgraceful episodes in the town's raffish history. At this period—indeed for some centuries up to the early 1800's—smuggling was an activity not just winked at but sometimes participated in by many local worthies all along the south coast, and in Dorset as intensively as anywhere. On this occasion, a certain John Diamond with some accomplices bought two tons of tea in Guernsey and carried it to Poole in a cutter under a captain named William Johnson, who, to the fury of Diamond and the rest deposited his cargo in the custom house. The gang decided to take the tea by main force, to which end they assembled a body of 60 men and advanced on Poole like a small army, 30 of them as an assault force, and 30 left as scouts or sentries, or as a reserve in case of need. Headed by one, Thomas Kingsmill, they broke into the custom house late at night and made off with 37 cwt. of tea, leaving all other goods where they lay. Laden as they were, and heavily armed, they galloped away with little attempt at concealment, and next morning rode through Fordingbridge in full view of a crowd, a foolhardy proceeding which speaks volumes for the usual attitude of country folk at the time to the activities of smugglers. It was not merely that people's sympathies lay with the law-breakers. They were also afraid. One witness of the cavalcade through Fordingbridge informed against them, and was murdered, together with a Southampton customs official in whose company he was on his way to a Justice of the Peace in Chichester. Later ten of the men concerned, including Kingsmill, were hanged for these crimes.

Across the road from the custom house, altogether less dignified and contrasting cheerfully with it, stands the harbour office, a small colonnaded building, dumpy and domestic, and bearing high up on the eastern end a brightly painted relief portrait and the inscription, 'Benjamin Skutt, Mayor, An. 1727. Jn. Awbrey Fecit.'

Several nearby warehouses still in use date from the eighteenth and early nineteenth centuries. On one can be seen a plaque recording that Charles X of France landed nearby on his way to exile at Lulworth Castle after the revolution of 1830. Inland, not far from the quay are the old Mansion House, in red brick, and embellished with a splendid porch, and opposite, just across the narrow street, St. James' Church, the parish church of Poole, a plain, handsome, no-nonsense building of 1820. Behind it the vicarage stands, prim, be-shrubbed, and decent. The immediate vicinity of the church has still a strongly eighteenth-century air mitigated with neglect.

Much of the old town of Poole wears dilapidation like a garment, patched in places, where some merchant's house recalling the town's prosperity at the height of the Newfoundland trade in the eighteenth century has been maintained or reclaimed from the decay around it. Such is, for instance, No. 67, Market Street, now used as part of the municipal college. No. 46 and No. 20 Market Street, are also worth examining, so is Joliffe House in West Street. In the High Street, by its junction with South Road, the Westminster Bank building and not far off a fine example of Georgian red brick with a semi-circular porch, used now as furniture showrooms, lord it over their mean surroundings. The only eighteenth-century public building still extant and in use is the former Guildhall, in Market Street, a long building in red brick with portico, stone pediment and dressings and two elegantly curved staircases. It stands regally in the centre of the street, crowned with a cupola, the largely contemporary buildings on either side deferentially withdrawn like courtiers.

The southern end of the High Street still has something of the same period, despite the squalor of its shop windows. To the east bulldozers have razed the past for partial replacement with eleven-storey blocks of flats and car parks. To the west, there are still glimpses of history, small alleys and odd entrances which invite exploration and all too often disappoint with a view of dereliction—dustbins, carcases of long immobile cars, and piles of bricks. There are street names—Dear Hay Lane, Barber's Piles, Towngate Street, Hunger Hill—like snatches of an old story.

Indeed, Poole's history goes back further than the century of Pope and Johnson. Most of what remains of old Poole stems from that time and the visitor feels that Poole has an eighteenth-century heart. But her origin lies 600 years before.

Poole does not appear in the Doomsday Book, though Hamworthy does—just across one of the Harbour's numberless inlets, joined to Poole by a bridge and centuries of symbiosis. But in 1248 Poole not only existed, but extracted a charter from the Lord of the Manor of Canford, in whose demesne it lay, on a small peninsula with an easily defensible narrow neck. This lord, William Longespée, was a son of Ela, Countess of Salisbury and her husband, also called William Longespée (i.e. Longsword), an illegitimate son of Henry II and Rosamund Clifford.

The younger Longespée succeeded to some of his father's estates, but not his title, which belonged only to his mother's husband. Since she remained a widow, and outlived both her son and his successor, neither of them was Earl of Salisbury, though they did hold the Manor of Canford, among others. Now Longespée II wished to go crusading, and the people of Poole knew he needed money for his expedition. They took the opportunity, therefore, to buy their charter, and hence the right to some self-government, at the bargain price of 70 marks. The town has lived by commerce, legitimate and otherwise, ever since.

A century after the granting of this first charter, she seems to have flourished. She provided ships for the king's service, and she was bold enough to petition in 1341 for 'all customs and liberties which the burgesses of Melcombe have, by charter, had granted to them by the kings of England'. Some kind of boundary dispute seems to have occurred at this time, for in a curious document dating from 1364, known as the Winchelsea Certificate, the Mayor and Corporation of Winchelsea assert that they recognise the boundaries of Poole to be those established by a royal enquiry in 1342. The mayor of Poole is still by courtesy 'Admiral of the Port', and periodically beats the water bounds detailed in this declaration.

At the turn of the century we meet the redoubtable Harry Page, or Paye, called by the French and Spaniards Arripay, a buccaneer of distinction, and Vice Admiral of the Cinque Ports Navy. He seems not to have been a native of Poole, but he owned property there, his brother lived there, and he used Poole Harbour as the base for his expeditions. He was obviously a formidable character, and is said to have brought back 120 prizes from one foray alone. To such a pitch did he goad the king's enemies that a Franco-Spanish force tried in 1406 to eliminate him by destroying him like a beast in its lair. They sailed into the Harbour, landed at Poole, burned and killed, despite spirited resistance by the townsfolk, and made off with presumably lighter hearts, having disburdened themselves of at least part of a debt of honour. Paye's brother was killed in this affair, but the pirate-in-chief was unscathed.

The town can show still some scanty remains from Arripay's hey-day. On Paradise Street, just near the Quay stands the substantial, grey but not unfriendly, stone pile of what is variously called Scalpen's Court, or the Old Town House. Part of this building appears to date from the latter part of the fourteenth century, though most of what now stands is perhaps a hundred years later. The house has been identified with very fair probability as one singled out by John Leland, the Tudor traveller and antiquary, who visited Poole in the reign of Henry VIII, as 'a fair town house of stone by the Quay'. It was probably used as a Guildhall until 1572, when another was built in Fish Street (which no longer exists), itself to be replaced by the one already referred to in Market Street. Having passed through many occupations and served several functions it had become a noisome slum by the twentieth century, but 40 years ago it was rescued and largely restored. It is a construction of two storeys built round a stone flagged courtyard, and backed by a garden nowadays carefully maintained. Appropriate items from the town's museum are displayed there, and it is also used for small exhibitions.

Nearby stands another grey stone building of comparable antiquity—the so-called Town Cellars, which early records call significantly 'The Woolhouse'. The date of its construction is unknown, but fairly obviously it originated in the early fifteenth century. Some of its features, particularly its stone-mullioned windows with pointed head and tracery, suggest by association some ecclesiastical purpose, but this was simply the fashion of building at the time, and there is no evidence of any connection with the church. It was originally 120 feet long, but in the last century it was cut into two unequal parts by the construction of Thames Street. Poole's third main relic of the time of Henry IV is the almshouses of St. George in Church Street, but they are very much restored and altered.

In the next century Poole had become a place of real importance, and in 1568 Queen Elizabeth created the town a county in its own right, giving it a dignity upon which its successive Mayors were very apt to stand. It was indeed during this reign that the waywardness of Poole's authorities reached its apogee. The Mayors of Poole regarded some of the fruits of the piracy that the local seamen practised as more or less their perquisites. Having their own Court of Admiralty and insisting on their rights, they were often at loggerheads with the Queen's officers, the Vice-Admirals of Dorset and of Purbeck, and stood in an excellent position to accept favours from the buccaneers whose activities the Queen was trying to curb.

In one particularly flagrant case in 1584 a pirate of Melcombe Regis (now part of Weymouth), one Bartholomew Belpitt, brought charges in Poole against eight rivals on the ground that as an innocent trader he had been 'spoiled at the seas' by them. One of them threatened publicly to incriminate the Poole authorities if he were condemned, and was judiciously acquitted together with three others. Although the Queen's Commissioners for the reform of piracy ordered the Mayor of Poole to bring the other four accused before them, he defiantly committed them to gaol in Dorchester, denying the Commissioners' jurisdiction in his town, and refusing a summons himself to appear before them. The riposte was an allegation that the Mayor and some of his fellow citizens had bought a richly-laden pirate prize, and had allowed the pirates not only to land at Poole but to steal a vessel in which they sailed off to commit further felony on the high seas.

Though the outcome of this squabble was inconclusive, there can be no doubt that Poole was pretty heavily committed to un-fettered free enterprise. Moreover, it was more than normally unwilling to participate in such fundamental co-operative ac-tivity as the defence of the realm. In 1577 Poole refused to pay a tax laid on it for mustering a mere 30 soldiers, and this despite its undoubted wealth at the time. In the year of the Armada, 1588, it pleaded poverty as an excuse for not sending the two ships that the Privy Council demanded of it to serve under Drake, the Mayor having the superb effrontery to allege that the town was in decline owing to the pirates of Studland. As a result the town provided no ships at all (in contrast to Lyme and Weymouth, who sent two each) for the fleet which fought the Armada. One Poole vessel was there, however—a volunteer, whose Catholic master had accepted a gift of £10 from a Catholic gentleman of Ham-worthy not to fight. Her captain, Henry Trenchard of Lytchett Minster in East Dorset, realising his half-heartedness, had him replaced at the last moment.

During the Civil War, Poole declared for Parliament, and was immediately isolated, since this part of the country favoured the King. In 1643 a Royalist army under the Earl of Crawford be-sieged the town without much success. It came to the Earl's notice, however, that a certain Captain Francis Sydenham was open to consider betraying the stronghold for cash and a pardon. On receipt of £40 from the Royalists it was agreed that when Sydenham was captain of the watch the town gate (roughly on the site of the present railway station) should be left unlocked, and on an agreed signal the Earl should enter with his army. Crawford sent a further £100, and impatiently awaited the moment of decision. It arrived. The gate indeed lay open. As Sydenham gave his signal 500 triumphant Cavaliers poured through the ingloriously breached defences to kill and burn for King Charles. But the advantage of surprise lay in fact with the defenders. Once the enemy were inside the walls the gate closed, and a destructive hail of bullets poured from all sides into the Royalist force. Crawford himself somehow escaped, but most of his men were killed, and Poole never fell to the King. On the contrary, it was an army based on Poole which effected the conquest of east Dorset for Parliament, and it was the Governor of Poole who commanded the force which in 1646 took Corfe Castle through a true act of treachery.

After the Restoration royalism became fashionable again, and King Charles II had an enthusiastic welcome on a visit undertaken in 1665 to avoid the plague in London. Of this period there survives a visible trace in the form of a plaque on a building of glass and steel in Castle Street. It records the fact that the Rev. John Wesley, the grandfather of a more famous namesake, was imprisoned 'for conscience' sake' in the gaol under the Guildhall which at that time stood nearby and has now utterly vanished. It reminds us that 'good King Charles' golden days' were of baser metal for Dissenting clergy who offended against the Clarendon Code.

Apart from this sobering notice the Tudor and Stuart periods have left little to be seen in the town today. In West Street there remain the almshouses of Richard Rogers, a Poole man who made money in leather in London, and as an act of piety endowed this foundation in 1604. It is not as he left it, for in 1852 it was added to, and the whole building was restored in 1927. Elsewhere there are pieces of old building still in use—here a slab of 400-year-old wall, there a fireplace of three centuries ago, and perhaps a cellar, filled in Shakespeare's day with Heaven knows what—but generally, the sixteenth and seventeenth centuries are ill-represented in the town.

Thanks to its favoured position on the Harbour shore, Poole avoided the decline that afflicted Lyme Regis and Weymouth after the excitements of the seventeenth century. Even during the years after the wars with Napoleon, when the Newfoundland trade dwindled and the new manufacturing industries were shifting the fulcrum of Britain's economy to the north and midlands, Poole retained fair importance as a centre for the distribution of the pottery clay found in various places in the district. Much of it came across the Harbour in the first place, loaded into barges at Wareham or one of the wooden jetties which still survive on the southern shore, such as Pikes Wharf and Goathorn Pier, for trans-shipment at Poole Quay. By 1840, indeed, nearly a third of all the pottery made in England was manufactured from clay shipped out of Poole. This trade again has shrunk though the area still owes some of its economic significance to it, and to the actual manufacture here of fine pottery.

Although as a port Poole now must be called minor, its current prosperity rests on various light industries and its virtues as a holiday resort. But even today the Quay still draws its flocks of visitors who perch their cars along it like birds on telegraph wires, gazing at the ships loading or discharging cargo, or just riding at anchor, and the yachts and small motor vessels that pass up and down the channel leading to the marshy inlet called Holes Bay. Across this channel a bridge has been thrown to carry traffic to Hamworthy, now a rather dull suburb, though it has been inhabited more or less continuously since pre-Roman times. The Romans built a road from it to Badbury Rings. Part of this road is to be seen and walked (at Corfe Mullen) and for a long distance it forms the eastern boundary of the borough. There was a plausible enough tradition that the Purbeck marble for Salisbury Cathedral was carried along it.

A more attractive sight from the Quay to the south-east is the long green slab of Brownsea Island, the largest of the several islands of sand and heath in the Harbour, and the destination of a pleasant trip in a boat from the Quay, or (a much shorter journey) from Sandbanks.

In 1154 Henry II granted the right to all wrecks of the sea at

Brownsea to Cerne Abbey, whose monks built a chapel on the island. After the Dissolution Brownsea reverted to the Crown, and Henry VIII, concerned as he was with coastal defence, established a small gun castle at the eastern end where it commanded the entrance to Poole Harbour. The present castle, a nineteenth-century gentleman's residence, stands on the same site, but very little of the original building survives. During the sixteenth century Poole was expected to supply a garrison, arms and ammunition for whom were the responsibility of the Crown. In 1576, however, Elizabeth made her favourite, Sir Christopher Hatton, Vice-Admiral of Purbeck, including Brownsea, where authority was delegated to a certain Christopher Anketill to the intense irritation of the Mayor of Poole. His privileges were, he felt, usurped, and his bribes from the local pirates and smugglers were now intercepted and pocketed by Anketill's henchmen. In fact the new masters levied a toll on the ferry across the harbour mouth and generally harried the lawful and unlawful activities of the local worthies. Despite this the Privy Council was told in 1588 that the fortifications of Brownsea were 'indifferent and of no use', unless arms and artillery were provided. In the Civil War Parliament garrisoned and fortified the island in earnest.

By the time of the Restoration the island had come into the possession of Sir Robert Clayton, a Lord Mayor of London, who reopened the copperas workings which had been operative in the previous century, and which were not finally closed until about 1700.

The present buildings on the island are largely relics of the nineteenth century, which saw its purchase in 1852 by a certain Col. William Waugh under the mistaken impression derived from his wife, who was an amateur geologist, and erroneously confirmed both by an acknowledged expert and an engineer, that it contained workable deposits of clay suitable for making fine porcelain. This unfortunate error bankrupted Waugh, but before the crash he rebuilt the castle, constructed the church, including in it some oak panelling from Richard III's council chamber at Crosby Hall, in London, reclaimed marshland at the eastern end of the island, and put up cottages and a school house for his clay workers and their families.

As everyone knows, Scouts the world over have a special regard for Brownsea as the birthplace of their movement, because Baden-Powell held his first camp there, for about 20 boys, in 1907. Since 1962, when it came into the care of the National Trust, its significance for the rest of us has been enhanced, and we can not only gaze at it from the Harbour shores, or sail round it at a respectful distance. We can walk its rhododendron thickets and heaths, we can bathe from its beaches, admire the shimmering peacocks in the parkland round its church, and as an especial treat if the weather is fair enjoy Shakespeare in the open air theatre of an August evening. If none of that pleases us, we may well visit it none the less for the nature reserve established on the north-east quarter.

Out of Poole three roads lead into Dorset. One is for Wareham and Dorchester; one by way of the ferry over the harbour mouth, from Sandbanks to Shell Bay, leads directly into the Isle of Purbeck; and the third runs to Wimborne Minster. Along the Wimborne road it comes as a surprise to discover that one is still in the borough of Poole as far as the bridge over the Stour, fully five miles as the crow flies from the Quay. The site of the old manor of Canford, at Canford Magna, which was the fount of Poole's autonomy 700 years ago, lies a little way downstream. Longespée's dwelling has long gone but a fragment known misleadingly as John of Gaunt's kitchen, dates from the fifteenth century and is incorporated in Canford School, a largely nineteenth-century building. The red sandstone church, parts of which are Norman, was savagely restored in 1876, but still has a little atmosphere, while Canford Magna itself consists partly of a pleasant group put up in the nineteenth century by the Guest family, the then lords of the Longespée's domain, as ideal homes for the working classes.

The land here is no longer the sour heath of Poole and its immediate hinterland, but the lush alluvial soil of the Stour valley, with green flat fields and a sense of comfort. Wimborne Minster lies on the far side of the river, wearing the air of genial permanence characteristic of old towns by the banks of rivers in shallow valleys. Old it assuredly is, older indeed than its narrow approaches or even its variegated and venerable Minster suggest.

Traces have been found here of Roman occupation, and inside the Minster church is a fragment of a tessellated pavement *in situ* in the nave, visible through a protective glass panel. A pediment was also found during restoration work, indicating along with other finds at least habitation and probably a temple. Immediately one wonders whether the church was deliberately built here to Christianise a pagan shrine, like for example the one not far off at Knowlton. The earliest known date in Wimborne's history is A.D. 705, when King Ine of Wessex gave a site by the confluence of the Allen and the Stour to his sister, Cuthburga, for a monastery, of which she became the abbess. St. Cuthburga (for she was canonised) died in 720, and the present Minster church is dedicated to her. In 871 King Alfred's elder brother, Ethelred, killed in battle against the Danes, was buried in the monastery church, and a brass 600 years later was placed in the Minster recording his sepulture, but wrong as to the date by two years. The brass is still there, but the actual site of Ethelred's tomb is unknown. By the year of King Alfred's death, 901, the town was fortified, for the rebel Ethelwald occupied it against King Edward the Elder, who encamped at Badbury Rings threatening to give battle. Ethelwald, however, thought better of the enterprise and stole away by night to Northumbria, whence he fled to Normandy. With an army of Vikings he returned to England and to death in battle at Bury St. Edmunds.

The Saxon monastery was destroyed, probably by the Danes in the reign of Ethelred the Unready, but by 1066 a new foundation had been created. At this time the area round about formed part of the royal demesnes of Wessex, and throughout the Middle Ages successive monarchs showed interest in the affairs of Wimborne. Thus in 1238 Henry III declared the Deanery of Wimborne to be a special chapel of his own, and 80 years later Edward II declared the Minster his free chapel, so that it stood outside the jurisdiction of the see of Salisbury, in which it lay. In 1223-4 it had been made a college of secular canons.

The Deans who governed this college included among others less noteworthy several names of significance outside Wimborne itself. John de Kirkby, Dean in 1265, was a worldly priest notorious for his avarice. Archbishop Peckham refused to approve his appointment to the see of Rochester in 1285, but he did become Bishop of Ely in the following year. In 1485 the Dean was William Smyth, who in 1493 became Dean of St. Stephen's, Westminster, and then bishop successively of Lichfield and Lincoln. From 1500-3 he was Chancellor of Oxford University. He was co-founder of Brasenose College and also a member of the Royal council. The most distinguished of all was Reginald Pole, who became Dean in 1518, in his nineteenth year. He became later a cardinal, and was Archbishop of Canterbury under Bloody Mary. He was even elected to the Papacy, which office, however, he refused.

After the Reformation the government of the Minster became entangled with the fortunes and regulation of the Grammar School, which had been founded in 1509 by Lady Margaret Beaufort, the mother of Henry VII, and the recipient, as a gift from her royal son, of the manor of Canford. The Governors of the school after 1562, chosen from men of the parish, were to pay a rent to the Crown, as well as to maintain the Church and the schoolhouse and provide clergy and teachers. To enable them to meet their obligations the tithes were vested in them, but since they were themselves the main tithe-payers, and filled vacancies in their number by their own choice, the possibilities of corruption seem to have been equalled by the actualities. To make matters worse the Governors appointed and paid the presiding official of the only court before which the townsfolk could bring them to book. The results can be imagined. During the first part of the seventeenth century, moreover, governors and parishioners were at loggerheads on doctrine, the former favouring the Puritans and appointing divines of their own persuasion, the parishioners largely preferring their opponents. Moreover, it apears that the Governors neglected to keep the Minster and the priest's dwellings in repair.

The physical relics of this turbulent past form one of Dorset's particular treasures. All styles of architecture from the Conquest to the Reformation are fully represented in the Minster itself. Its massive and commanding Norman central tower, built of stone both grey and every shade of russet, despite the unfortunate crenellations, replacing a spire which fell in 1600, dominates the entire fabric, and the entire town centre. The grey west tower, pleasantly weathered, and dating from the late fifteenth century, stands to it as a lady to her knight. Inside, too, the great Norman piers of the crossing, with their round arches and their squat cushion capitals, seem to anchor the whole building. The Transitional arcades are elaborately decorated with chevron ornamentation, and the Early English presbytery has a three-light lancet window at the east end, the centre light filled with fifteenth-century Flemish glass. The transepts are partly Norman, the remoter aisles, north and south, were built in the fourteenth century and include some of the best Decorated work in the county. Over the vestry is a library of chained books given to the citizens of Wimborne by the Rev. William Stone in 1686. The most curious item is Sir Walter Raleigh's *History of the World* (1634), in 104 pages of which a hole has been burned, and repaired. Legend has it that the hole was burned by the carelessness of the satirist, Matthew Prior, who is also supposed to have effected the neat and laborious repairs, though the story may well be apocryphal. It is not even sure that Prior was a Wimborne man, though he probably was, the son of Dissenting parents (which would explain why no record of his baptism survives) and born in 1664.

Round the corner, in the Trinity Chapel, in a niche in the south wall is the tomb of one Anthony Ettricke (1623-1703), a gentleman of Holt (a dull village now, a few miles to the north), an antiquarian who contributed additions on Dorset to Camden's *Britannia*, and a man of law who, as Recorder of Poole, had the distinction of committing the Duke of Monmouth upon his capture near Horton after Sedgemoor. 'Towards the end of his life,' Hutchins says of him, 'he grew very humoursome, phlegmatic, and credulous,' and in a moment of displeasure with the people of Wimborne (no one knows the cause) swore that he would be buried neither in their church nor out of it, neither in their ground nor on it. He kept his oath by arranging to occupy the very cavity where he remains. His coffin bears the date of his death, 1703, rather clumsily and obviously altered from 1693, in which year he had prepared to die, convinced by some misleading premonition.

A more splendid but less curious monument, is the tomb in the presbytery of John Beaufort, Duke of Somerset (d. 1444), and his wife, Margaret. Their daughter, Margaret, Countess of Richmond, was the foundress of the Grammar School. The couple lie in effigy side by side on the tomb, she on his right, clasping his right hand with hers.

In the west tower, high up on the south wall, is an astronomical clock said to have been made by a monk of Glastonbury in 1320. It still works, and operates the mechanism by which the hours are struck. The quarters are struck by another mechanism, connected to a little red-coated Grenadier who stands on the outside of the tower giving much pleasure to passing children every 15 minutes, by behaving as though on a parade ground.

In the busy streets round about the Minster can be found a fair number of old houses, some of them half-timbered and dating from the sixteenth century. The oldest and most interesting is the so-called Priest's House, which has a partly Georgian front, but a strongly sixteenth-century atmosphere inside. It is used as a museum now, containing a small, pleasantly presented, miscellany of items from Wimborne's past, while at the back is a serene garden dominated by a venerable mulberry tree. In the Cornmarket stands the George Inn, on whose site there has been a building devoted to the same purpose at least since 1524. The Market Square has a number of Georgian buildings, which are surpassed, however, by those in the wide street called West Borough, where the eighteenth century can still be almost experienced despite the parked cars and vans.

Children enjoy the model town next to the Cornmarket, where the centre of Wimborne, including the Minster, is reproduced on Lilliputian scale, but unpeopled, as though at daybreak on a summer day. If they have read *The Borrowers Aloft* their imagination will be ripe for the experience.

Leaving the old centre of the town, except by two of the three routes to Blandford, one must cross a bridge. There is a tiny one east of the Minster over the little river Allen; a fine one reconstructed in 1793 over the Stour at Oakley, where the river forms the boundary with Poole; a better one still, known as Julian's Bridge, probably after a certain Walter Julian, again over the Stour on the A 31, taken over by the County in 1633, and repaired at intervals since, and another small one over the Allen on the Cranborne road. They are all quite inadequate for modern traffic. By the Badbury Rings road, along which there is no bridge to cross, stands the little chapel of St. Margaret, with a cluster of old cottages, remnants of the medieval Leper Hospital. It was founded before 1240, and in 1241 Pope Innocent IV granted an indulgence of 50 years and 160 days to all its benefactors subject to the recital of a prescribed number of Paternosters and Aves. The chapel, itself dating from the thirteenth century, has been recently subjected to a restoration which leaves it looking raw and far from medieval.

Of the villages round about several are worth a visit. Lytchett Matravers and Corfe Mullen both have attractive brown sandstone churches of some interest, that of Corfe Mullen incorporating an Early English east window, and an attractive plastered barrel roof with gay carved bosses. The church at Lytchett Matravers lies some way from the road, half surrounded by trees, and looking across gently rounded low hills into the heart of Dorset. It has some features dating from the thirteenth century, some sixteenth-century glass, and, in the chancel, a small brass to Thomas Pethyn, a vicar who died about 1470, and is represented in a shroud, which envelops him in the most becoming and elegant curves and loops.

It is also the burial place of John, Baron Matravers, from whose family, as lords of the manor from the time of William the Conqueror, the village derives its name. He fought at Bannockburn, where he was taken prisoner, and in 1319 he was knight of the Shire for the Parliament held at York. He was later in rebellion against the domination of Edward II by the Despencers, and had to flee after the battle of Borough Bridge. Having returned on the accession of Edward III he was appointed keeper of the dethroned Edward II at Berkeley Castle, where he was probably, with his fellow-gaoler, Sir John Gourney, responsible for that unfortunate king's murder. He died in 1365, and a memorial slab remains in the nave.

Both these villages are diffuse and unplanned, much altered by the building of commuter bungalows. They both stand on a narrow strip of London clay which borders the heath like a lining between it and the chalk, and influences the character of the villages that it contains in that they have less shape and, to be frank, character, than those on the chalk uplands. Corfe Mullen, indeed, sprawls into the heathland proper, as do some of the other villages on the clay belt, which stretches to the area east of Cranborne.

North-west of Lytchett is the great park of Charborough, which contains the folly (a landmark for miles) that Hardy used as the astronomer's tower in *Two on a Tower*. Back on the alluvial land of the Stour valley, the river may be crossed by an ancient bridge at Sturminster Marshall, and a country road followed north to the Iron Age fort at Badbury Rings. This great earthwork stands squat and enormous on high chalky ground overlooking the Stour valley and commanding views as far as the hills of Purbeck and Cranborne Chase. It is a shallow cone, furrowed by three steep ramparts and their ditches, and crowned with a dense wood. It has been suggested that Badbury was *Mons Badonicus*, the scene of King Arthur's victory over the Saxons, but the evidence is as nebulous as the battle itself. Traces have been found here of Bronze Age occupation, and the fort as we see it is the work of Veneti, probably in the first century B.C., who designed it for defence in slingstone warfare, with an outer rampart a mile in circumference. A nodal point of Roman roads, the setting for the Court of the Hundred of Badbury, the intended assembly place for a division of the Dorset defence forces at the time of the Armada, and the scene of a gathering of the Clubmen in 1645, the Rings today are a week-end playground for the citizenry. But at dusk, or during the week, or otherwise out of season, left to the south-west wind and its noisy play with tree and bush, the Rings and all their associations have a poetry quite their own.

The northernmost of the three routes from Wimborne to Blandford Forum passes them on the south-west, in this part flanked by two rows of beech trees extending for two miles westward from the main entrance to the park of Kingston Lacy. They were planted about a hundred years ago, but the story that there are 365 trees on each side, one for each day of the year, has no foundation. As its name suggests, Kingston Lacy was originally royal property, taking its second element from the family name of John de Lasey, Constable of Chester, and one of the 25 barons chosen to ensure the observance of Magna Carta. He was granted the manor in 1229, being created Earl of Lincoln in 1232. The last of the de Lacys to hold Kingston was Alice, John's great-granddaughter, who married an Earl of Lancaster in 1294, and took the manor to him as part of her inheritance on the death of her father in 1311. She must have been a person of turbulent character. In 1318 either she was kidnapped by the Earl of Warrenne, a favourite of Edward II's or she deserted her husband for him. Then a lawsuit appears in the records involving a claim by a hunch-back called Richard Martin, who alleged that she had been married to him before her espousal to Lancaster, and claimed the earldoms of Salisbury and Lincoln in her right. She returned to Lancaster, who proceeded to rebel against the king, but was defeated and executed in 1322. Alice married twice more, but survived her three (or was it four?) husbands until 1348, and on her death, childless, the manor reverted to the crown. It passed by purchase in 1636 to Sir John Bankes, attorney-general of Charles I. Bankes was the chief prosecutor in the case of John Hampden, and in 1641 became Lord Chief Justice of the Court of Common Pleas. It was his brave wife (his widow after 1644) who defended Corfe Castle against the attacks of the Roundheads, and it was his second son, Ralph, who had the present house of Kingston Lacy built for him in 1663-5 by Sir Roger Pratt. The property has remained in the Bankes family ever since. Pratt built the house of brick, but in alterations from 1835-9 by Sir Charles Barry, it was faced with grey stone. It stands in superbly landscaped grounds, with wide lawns and spreading trees and contains a very rich collection of pictures. Fortunately, these and other splendours may be seen by the public frequently during the summer.

On the eastern edge of the estate is the hamlet of Pamphill, a particular favourite of my own for its essentially rural informality. Its green is as pretty a field for week-end cricket as you can imagine, it has a manor house of the late seventeenth century (built by the steward to Sir Ralph Bankes), it has scattered cottages, and it has the red brick building, still in use as a primary school, built in 1698 from a bequest by a certain Roger Gillingham for the establishment of a school and almshouses.

To the east of Wimborne, the villages on the heathland north of Bournemouth—Verwood, Ferndown, West Moors—are no more than dormitories for that monster on the coast. In the Stour valley West Parley and Longham are undergoing the same process of submergence, and only Hampreston has for the time being partially survived on its cul-de-sac, though without much individuality. Even its church, cruelly mishandled in the last century, lacks any noticeable atmosphere, despite the felicitously grotesque corbels in the chancel.

To the north of Wimborne, the road to Cranborne, after crossing the River Allen, climbs out of the river's narrow valley on to the chalk hills. Reached by a turning from the main road some way north of Hinton Parva is Chalbury, which as a village need not detain us, except for its small church, which is one of Dorset's most delightful. The fabric, mostly Early English and Decorated, retains its plaster inside and out. The interior is almost totally Georgian, with box pews, an imperious three-decker pulpit, and a west gallery. The entrance to the chancel is through an arch of wooden pillars. The place remains very obviously cared for and used, and has a vivacity quite lacking in some more pretentious ecclesiastical buildings. It stands on a hill a little more than 300 feet above sea level overlooking the flat, heathy plain of east Dorset, with Bournemouth in the far distance, and the hills of Purbeck and of Cranborne Chase to the south and north respectively.

One highly conspicuous object from Chalbury Hill is Horton Tower, built as an observatory in the eighteenth century and now a ruin. The village from which it takes its name, a bare mile from Chalbury, was once the site of an abbey, but has now little of interest except the former vicarage (which is all that remains of the eighteenth-century manor house) and the church itself, a grey stone, L-shaped building with a pyramidal roof to its tower. It was rebuilt about 1722, either by Vanbrugh, or an assiduous pupil, and contains a rather garish reredos of the period. Its monuments include an effigy in Purbeck marble of Sir Giles de Braose, who died in 1305, and another in Ham stone probably of his wife Beatrice.

The road north-west out of Horton crosses the Wimborne-Cranborne main road at the Horton Inn, a lonely building and quite a landmark on the brow of a bare hill where the fields are large and trees few. Moving still north-westward the road dips into the valley of the Allen, which it crosses by a medieval stone bridge, then climbs again to run along a chalk ridge to the Blandford-Salisbury road on Thickthorn Down. Crossing the main road (the A 354) and leaving Chettle on the west it continues through Farnham to the Wiltshire border near Tollard Royal. Following the county boundary round (on the map rather than literally) as far as the road from Cranborne to Martin, then coming south-west again through Cranborne back to the Horton Inn, one has perambulated a roughly square stretch of chalk upland, undulating gently, cut by three small streams, two of which are tributaries of the Allen, and one, the Cran, flows ultimately into the Moors River near Verwood. Within this square lie some of the most fascinating of Dorset's, perhaps even of Britain's pre-historic monuments, with some later ones of more than ordinary interest, countryside of unexpected and refreshing peace and remoteness, and villages hardly touched by the twentieth century. North of Farnham, Sixpenny Handley, and Woodyates, lie the hills and woods of Cranborne Chase, much of which lies outside Dorset, and much again, though in Dorset, outside the limits of this chapter. But here it must be mentioned as the site of some of the most important excavations of Pitt-Rivers, one of the founding fathers of British scientific archaeology.

The Hampshire boundary on the north-east side of our square is formed by Bokerly Dyke, an earthwork thrown up in late Roman times as a protection against incursions from the north-east. It snakes for four miles across downland that was open country at least as long ago as the Late Bronze Age, its flanks protected by woodland—the ancient forest of the Chase to the north, and woods on the clay strip edging the heathland to the south. It is a great rampart, its ditch on the Hampshire side, its top even now in places a good 20 feet from the bottom of the ditch, despite a millennium and a half of weathering and silting. It appears to have grown through three stages. The first, about A.D. 325-30 saw its beginning perhaps as a ranch boundary, then later in the fourth century it was used for military purposes and extended temporarily over the road from Badbury Rings to Old Sarum, and at last, at about the end of the century (possibly under the direction of Stilicho, 'the last of the Romans'), it was placed permanently athwart the road. It served its purpose as a defensive fortification for over a century, and remains impressive to this day.

Traversing the square not quite diagonally, but roughly from north-east to south-west, is the Roman road known in this area as Ackling Dyke. The modern Salisbury-Blandford road, a legacy of the turnpike system, following its line enters the county at Bokerly Junction, a point half a mile from the church-less village of Woodyates. A mile south-east it diverges from the Roman route, on Oakley Down, whence Ackling Dyke continues on its imperturbably straight way. For at least four miles, from Oakley Down to beyond Gussage Hill, the *agger*, or causeway, is in splendid condition, forming, according to L. V. Grinsell, 'the most magnificent stretch of Roman road in Britain'. The *agger* is six feet high, and between 40 and 50 feet wide at its base, and the ditches (now largely filled) roughly 84 feet apart. To walk along this stretch is an exhilarating experience to anyone with half an eye for country allied to a little historical imagination. The legions, the traders, the landowners, and the slaves and serfs, all travelled this very road, treading the stones which still lie below the rough turf that clothes them today, tramping on foot or rumbling in heavy carts, or luxuriously carried in litters over the bare hills and across the valleys, and past remnants of older cultures which they may have noticed, if at all, with superstitious awe or the idlest curiosity.

On Oakley Down, in a triangle formed by the modern main

road, Ackling Dyke, and the modern road from Cranborne to Sixpenny Handley, lies a group of round barrows of the Bronze Age, including half a dozen of the relatively unusual disc type— a round bank, with a ditch inside it, and within the circle a small, low mound. It seems a very fair guess that here is a cemetery for important people—kings and queens, or priests and priestesses, perhaps magical personages of the kind familiar nowadays from myth and anthropology who combined royal and hieratic duties.

On Gussage Hill is the site of an early settlement—Roman and pre-Roman—marked on the ground by banks and enclosures. This lies athwart a quite astonishing prehistoric construction, dated to Neolithic or early Bronze Age times, and known as the Dorset Cursus. It consists, or rather, consisted, of two parallel banks about 90 yards apart and six miles long, which extended from Bokerly Dyke, about a mile north of Pentridge, to Thickthorn Down, about a mile from Gussage St. Michael. Although for long stretches the Cursus has left no trace to the inexpert eye its course has been authoritatively plotted. It crosses Ackling Dyke on Wyke Down, and for a little distance here one bank about four feet high is to be seen and walked—as far, indeed, as the Cranborne to Sixpenny Handley road, and in short stretches on the other side of the road, where its discovery after a few hundred yards, however, is less easy since a forestry plantation has smothered it. At either end lies a group of long barrows, with one lying at right angles to its course. Two other long barrows lie across it on its journey—one near the settlement on Gussage Hill, and one in the plantation. Really, its magnitude takes one's breath away. R. J. C. Atkinson calculates that it enclosed 220 acres, and the volume of its earthworks amounted to six and half million cubic feet. Other cursuses, of course, are known, but this is by far the longest. To many people the cursus at Stonehenge is the most familiar, but the Dorset cursus is more than three times as long. And what was it for? We shall never know for certain. The long barrows that punctuate its course suggest an association with death and therefore religion. Perhaps it was a ceremonial way, perhaps a track for funeral games.

So much for the larger traces of antiquity in this part of the county. Among modern and thriving places the largest is Cranborne, once the site of an abbey, later the town where sat the Courts of the Chase which bears its name, but is now little more than a geographical expression. Formerly Cranborne Chase enclosed 700,000 acres, in a perimeter of 100 miles, bordered by the rivers Avon and Stour, and as late as the disafforestation of 1830 contained from 12,000 to 20,000 deer. The rights of the Chase—that is, the right to hunt over it—belonged after the Norman conquest to the Earls of Gloucester, but reverted to the Crown (i.e. the 'Chase' became a 'Forest') by the marriage of King John to an heiress of Gloucester. He divorced her after ascending the throne, but kept the Chase which, since he visited Cranborne 13 times, he clearly adored. It reverted to the House of Gloucester on his death. It again became a forest under Edward IV, to remain such until James I granted it to Robert Cecil. Later the rights passed to the Earls of Shaftesbury, then to the Pitt-Rivers family.

The Chase became in the eighteenth century the scene of frequent lawlessness. Its woodlands, then more extensive than now, offered cover and refuge to smugglers bringing contraband up from the coast. Its game proved an irresistible temptation to poachers, among whom were often included members of the neighbouring gentry, spurred on by envy of the Chase rights, and a certain lust for adventure, to violent, often bloody, and sometimes fatal escapades. The gamekeepers used all the means open to them to combat poaching, including of course appalling man-traps like those to be found in so many museums of rural life. Finally the Chase rights were abolished by Parliament in 1830 and the countryside became more wholesome.

The Manor of Cranborne belonged at Doomsday time to the Queen, from whom her son William Rufus inherited it. He gave it to Robert Fitz-Hamon, who founded the monastery of Tewkesbury. At that time the Abbey of Cranborne was already well over a century old, having been established by 980, but Fitz-

Hamon had the Abbot of Cranborne and his monks move to the newer seat, and Cranborne became a Priory of Tewkesbury. On Fitz-Hamon's death in 1107 his eldest daughter married Henry I's illegitimate son Robert, whom his father made Earl of Gloucester, and took Cranborne with her. In the following centuries it had a chequered and complicated history, until in 1603 James I gave it to Robert Cecil with whose descendants it has remained ever since.

It was this Robert Cecil, the first Earl of Salisbury, who built the manor house which stands today. Its core is a building of about fourteenth-century date, but between 1607 and 1611 it acquired its present Jacobean character. It is of grey stone, with porticoes of twisted columns, tall brick chimneys, and high windows with stone mullions and transoms. Its gardens, of formal grace, largely retain the layout of Montagu Jennings and the plant collector, John Tradescant, who designed them for Cecil. The public are occasionally allowed to enjoy them.

Close to the manor is the church, a gem of a building, predominantly thirteenth century with an impressive and high tower of 1440, a Norman doorway in the porch, an oak pulpit of about 1400, and medieval paintings on the south wall of the nave. It is lofty and spacious, and clearly appropriate to a place much more important than Cranborne is today. Among its monuments are several to the Stillingfleet family, including the seventeenth-century divine and controversialist of that name, and a good but anonymous Jacobean altar tomb with recumbent effigies of a lady and gentleman. A window to John Tregonwell, who died in 1885, deserves mention only because of the untrue statement, which I have found in three different guide books, that that gentleman was the founder of Bournemouth. This title belongs to his father, Lewis, who in 1810, a year before John's birth, built a house by the sea half way between Poole and Christchurch. A memorial tablet in the south aisle commemorates one Robert Smart, 'forty-four years a surgeon in the town', born 1771, died 1840, his wife who died aged 92 in 1867, and (horrifically) their five infant children who died in 1798, 1800, 1803, 1808, and 1817. There need be no more vivid illustration of the condition of medicine and mankind a century and a half ago. This after all was the family of a medical man.

Since Cranborne lies at the junction of several roads one has a choice of ways out. On the Verwood road, in a lush hollow scooped out of the clay, is Edmondsham, which has a much-restored, originally twelfth-century church and a manor house in grey stone, largely of 1589, with additions in the eighteenth century. A more rewarding visit may be paid to Wimborne St. Giles, reached circuitously by turnings off the roads to Sixpenny Handley or back to Wimborne Minster. It stands on a little stream feeding a mill pond, flowing, crystal clear and populous with trout under a discreet bridge into the park of St. Giles' House. Nearby the village stocks are carefully preserved. A green open space backed by handsome trees dominates the village, bordered on the east side by a block of seventeenth-century brick almshouses and the church, a building of flint and ashlar, the latter covered with a patina of pale green lichen like oxidised copper. Although the shell of the present church dates from 1732 (the architect may have been one of the Bastard family of Blandford Forum), after a fire which gutted the interior in 1908 it was magnificently, and no other word will do, refitted by Sir Ninian Comper to a monumental and airy plan, with a controlled lushness of detail.

It stands by the entrance to St. Giles' House, the seat of the Earls of Shaftesbury. The house was begun in 1650 to a design in the style of Inigo Jones, but not only was part of an older building used, but alterations and additions have subsequently changed its appearance and it has now much of the atmosphere one associates with the eighteenth and nineteenth centuries. Like Kingston Lacy it is well supplied with good pictures, and fine furniture, and *objets d'art* generally, and boasts in its wide garden a delicate little shell grotto dating from the eighteenth century.

4   *Kingston Lacy, the saloon*

The house was built for the first Earl, but the estate goes back to the Conquest, since when it has never changed hands by purchase. In the fifteenth century it came by marriage to Robert Ashley, whose descendant, Anthony Ashley, was Clerk to Elizabeth I's Privy Council, and secretary for war in the Cadiz expedition, for which he was knighted. He it was who built the almshouses by the church. He translated Lucas Waghenner's sea charts (the first known collection) from the Dutch, and is alleged to claim our especial gratitude for the introduction to this country of the cabbage. The elaborate and handsome monument in the church to him and his wife, which survived the fire of 1908, incorporates by the feet of the effigies what looks like a decayed medicine ball, and is said to represent a cabbage indeed.

Sir Anthony's daughter, Anne, married Sir John Cooper, of Rockbourne in Hampshire, by whom she was the mother of Sir Anthony Ashley-Cooper, who succeeded to the estate on his father's death in 1631 when he was only ten years old. On the outbreak of the Civil War he sided with the King, but in 1644, disgusted with breaches of faith by Charles, changed sides. Soon after he took some part in the local movement known as the Clubmen, who professing to be a Third Force in the State, demanded an end to the war and a general conciliation, but were suppressed by Cromwell on Hambledon Hill in 1645. Thereafter, Ashley-Cooper embraced the cause of Parliament wholeheartedly, but played some part in engineering the Restoration. In 1667 he became Chancellor of the Exchequer, and four years later Lord Chancellor and Earl of Shaftesbury.

Charles II visited St. Giles during this time, and the story is told that with a number of gentlemen of the neighbourhood he retired one evening after dinner to the cellar, as an appropriate site for bibulation. In the subsequent merriment Mr. Edward Hooper of Boveridge (near Cranborne) so excelled that the King knighted him on the spot, the entire company being drunk. In 1667 John Locke took up residence at St. Giles' House as physician and

5 *Wimborne St. Giles Church, from the south-west*

family tutor, among his charges the third Earl (1671-1713), the author of the *Characteristics of Men, Manners, Opinions, Times,* and as such the occupant of a niche in the history of moral philosophy.

The first Earl's brilliance led him into controversial ways. A member of the notorious Cabal, that secret cabinet whose influence on Charles II was thought so unfortunate, and satirised as Achitophel in Dryden's poem,

> *For close designs and crooked counsels fit,*
> *Sagacious, bold, and turbulent of wit,*

he subsequently crossed the plans of the Catholic Duke of York, and found himself in opposition. He was exiled in 1681 and two years later died in Holland, but when his embalmed body was brought to Poole, 'the gentlemen [of Dorset] out of their extraordinary regard to his memory, came uninvited and accompanied it to Wimborne St. Giles'.

The seventh Earl (1801-85) is the best known of the line, for his philanthropy and his advocacy of laws against the inhuman conditions of work and life among the labouring poor. The statue of Eros in Piccadilly Circus commemorates him, and so does a a tablet in the church at Wimborne St. Giles, but as one whose efforts may be said to have contributed to the beginning of the idea of the Welfare State he has a ubiquitous monument in modern Britain.

Just over a mile from Wimborne St. Giles near the Cranborne-Wimborne Minster road, where it is joined by the road from Brockington Farm, stands the ruin of Knowlton church. The fifteenth-century tower survives and so do most of the roofless Norman nave and chancel, all of grey or brown stone with bands of flint, like so many churches in east Dorset. A tiny church it was, and the village of which it was once the centre has disappeared, but for a farmhouse. It would rate no more than a passing reference if it were not situated, uniquely, in the centre of a Bronze Age henge, a circular rampart over a hundred yards across, with a ditch (because it was a sacred site) on the inside, to protect the world from the egress of malignant spirits. Nearby are traces of three other rings, and a number of round barrows, of which the largest, a tree-clad monster 20 feet high, stands in a field just to the east.

Clearly Knowlton was a place of importance 4,000 years ago, possibly a religious centre ranking in this part of the country only after Stonehenge and Avebury. Perhaps it kept its magical character, even its holiness, through successive occupations by Celt, Roman, and Saxon, until the arrival of Christianity. Then the monks, finding that the local people would not turn from the worship of Knowlton's deities, built their church right inside the sacred circle, either to exorcise its evil powers, or to persuade the pagans that what the old gods ruled the new God had expropriated. Whatever actually happened, the suggestion is that worship continued at Knowlton in one form or another from about 1800 B.C. until the medieval church was abandoned. This kind of religious continuity can be inferred in other places in Dorset and elsewhere, but only at Knowlton is the evidence so striking.

The church was once a chapel of ease to Horton and 'in 1650 it lay unfrequented for many years'. It was repaired and again used about 1735, but this cannot have continued for long, and permanent dereliction set in. At one time a fair was held here but by the eighteenth century this had been removed to Woodlands (where the parish church now has Knowlton's font). The evocative ruin remains, standing in its carefully mown green circle, attended by the giant barrow and a train of withered yews.

The Gussage villages—Gussage All Saints, Gussage St. Michael, and Gussage St. Andrews—will attract attention if only because of their names. They all, in fact, have a certain charm, remote, quiet, and in keeping with the highly individual associations of the countryside of which they are part. A stream, accompanied by a pleasant country road runs down their valley in the chalk hills and past their flinty churches to join the Allen east of Knowlton. Gussage St. Andrew, cut off from its sisters by the Blandford-Salisbury road, is the smallest and most interesting. It consists of a cottage or two, a farm house, and a tiny church, which is Norman and Early English in style, has a fish for a weathervane, and some medieval wall paintings.

Not far off are Farnham, where Pitt-Rivers established his museum of archaeology and anthropology, and to the south-west the village of Chettle, a nondescript collection of brick, thatch, and corrugated iron, with a church of which the Victorians (as so regrettably often) left only the fifteenth-century tower unspoilt. Chettle House, of red brick with ashlar dressings, was designed by Thomas Archer about 1710, and contains some reliefs by Alfred Stevens, whose father was responsible for the decoration of the drawing-room. Although the house is now divided into flats, much of it may be seen by the public. The Chafin family, who built it, were Wardens of Cranborne Chase and the last of their line, the Rev. William Chafin (1731-1818) wrote a book of anecdotes of the Chase, when he was too old any more to enjoy the more active pleasures it offered.

North from Farnham, at Woodcutts, near the Wiltshire boundary, are the remains of a Romano-British village excavated in detail by Pitt-Rivers in 1884. The banks and ditches cover about four acres, and there are two wells which the General marked with headstones recording not only their depth (respectively 188 feet and 136 feet) but also the fact that in the deeper one he found a bucket and in the other nothing.

Perhaps it is sad to end a chapter with one of the county's dullest villages, but Sixpenny Handley must be mentioned because of its name, which fascinates everyone. It has nothing to do with money. Its origins lie in two Hundreds, Sexpena and Hanlega, which were united, and whose names were technically corrupted but obviously improved. The village fabric fails lamentably to fulfil the expectations of rural delight aroused by this result, and some have thought it the ugliest village in Dorset. Perhaps it is, but many counties would be happier if they could show no more offensive place than this.

CHAPTER THREE

The South-east

Poole is the only town on the harbour which bears its name, but at a much earlier stage of the silting which began many centuries ago the main settlement in this part of the county, and the only port of any significance, was Wareham. It lies now more than a mile from the shore, between the Frome and the Piddle, which flow into the Harbour within half a mile of each other. Although small boats from Poole make their way, freighted with holiday makers, up the reedy Frome to the little quay, commerce forsook Wareham a long time ago, and it disappears from the records as a port after 1347. At that time it still had enough wealth and importance to supply Edward III with three ships and 59 men for the siege of Calais.

In Saxon times Wareham had a priory founded by St. Aldhelm and some fortifications, which failed to save it from the Danes, for they sacked it in 876. In the reign of Athelstan it recovered, but suffered in Danish raids again in 998 and 1015. The great earthworks which still make three sides of a square about the town were probably thrown up as a defence against these Danish forays, and they were used again in the twelfth-century Barons' Wars, for in 1138 Robert de Lincoln seized Wareham for Matilda, only to lose it four years later, when Stephen devastated it.

Something remains of the eleventh-century town, for part of the church of St. Martin, perched on the wall where the road from Poole breaches it, dates from this period. According to tradition St. Aldhelm built a church here in the seventh century, but the earliest parts of the present building are only barely pre-Norman, and most of it dates from the twelfth and thirteenth centuries. It is a sprightly near-millennarian, and, after a period of disuse was re-dedicated in 1936. During restoration work at this time some medieval wall painting was uncovered, and in the north aisle was placed a splendid recumbent effigy of Lawrence of Arabia, carved by Eric Kennington.

The decline of Wareham was probably due to the silting up of the river estuaries, and the synchronous rise of Poole, so that in the later Middle Ages it became a backwater. At one time it had eight churches, of which only three survive, one of them (Holy Trinity) now disused. The parish church, at the southern end of the town, was savaged like so many Dorset churches by the Victorians, but has some interesting relics, including a leaden font of the twelfth century, some engraved stones apparently of the sixth or seventh century, and a Saxon stone coffin traditionally associated with King Edward the Martyr. John Hutchins (1698-1773), the historian of the county, was rector here from 1744 until his death. He had already begun the monumental work, on which all writers on Dorset's past must still lean, while occupying the living of Melcombe Horsey from 1733, and he died just before the publication of the first edition. He is described as 'a sound divine' who lacked 'eminence as a preacher', a characterisation which every reader of his painstakingly erudite volumes can imagine to have been accurate.

During the Civil War Wareham began on the side of Parliament, but changed hands several times until in 1644 Sir Anthony Ashley-Cooper finally took it by storm. The question of razing it was considered, Cooper believing that 'there can be no argument against the demolishing it, being extremely mean built and the inhabitants almost all dreadful malignants [i.e. Royalists]; besides, the keeping it will certainly starve more honest men than the destroying it will undo knaves'.

It was none the less spared and destruction came not by war, but by fire, to which Dorset towns in the seventeenth and eighteenth centuries were horribly prone. In 1762 much of the town was burned, 150 properties being lost. This fire, incidentally, almost cost us Hutchins' history, his manuscript being saved only by the exertions of his wife, since the Rector himself was away from home that day. Much of Wareham now dates from the time of rebuilding after that disaster. Within the old ramparts, which enclosed the entire town until the twentieth century, the streets are laid out in a gridiron pattern, based on two main streets which intersect at right angles in the centre. Many eighteenth-century buildings survive, and the southern half particularly of the old town has some streets of quiet elegance. The quay, by the modern bridge over the Frome, has a good group in red brick, and downstream the river washes the foot of the garden (sometimes open to the public) of the old Priory, an attractive Tudor house. The earthworks and walls may be walked and the view over the twin river valleys from the northwest corner admired.

This view indeed reveals one reason for Wareham's attraction for the Vikings. It was a gateway to the interior up-river, and conversely commanded the routes to the sea from the valley settlements. Looking south from the Frome bridge one can understand the other reason, too, for beyond the flat, bare heathland which in places approaches the very banks of the stream, is the range of steep chalk hills which shield the southern part of the Isle of Purbeck. Wareham commands the road to the gateway through them, Corfe Castle.

North-westward a straight road leads over the heath a mile or more from the left bank of the Piddle almost directly to Bere Regis, where the roads to Dorchester from Poole and Wimborne meet. 'A little one-eyed, blinking sort o' place', one of Hardy's characters calls it, while Sir Frederick Treves, another Dorset man, described it as 'a dull village adrift in a duller country'. Well, yes. And one might add that modern traffic has not caused it to blossom.

6 *St. Giles House, Wimborne St. Giles, the White Hall*

Yet it is the Kingsbere-sub-Greenhill of Hardy's Wessex, the ancestral burying place of the D'Ubervilles, a name which Hardy adapted only a little from that of the real family of the Turberviles whose ancestor Sir Payne de Turbervile (Sir Pagan D'Urberville in Hardy) actually came with the Conqueror. And anyone who makes a pilgrimage to Bere because of the story of Tess Durbeyfield may go into the church and see the chapel in the south aisle under which the real Turberviles are buried. Almost certainly, though, it is the ornate and elaborate roof which will make the first and strongest impression on him. From each truss a pair of Apostles, in fifteenth-century costume overlooks the congregation, and at the east end a large boss is carved to represent a face said to be that of Cardinal Morton, who gave the roof in 1475. Morton, born in Bere about 1420, and educated at Cerne Abbey, in 1461 became Rector of the neighbouring parish of Bloxworth. As Henry VII's Chancellor from 1487 he is remembered as the deviser of 'Morton's Fork', the argument according to which a man who spent little was taxed on the grounds that he must have been able to save, while one who spent freely was likewise taxed, because he obviously had money to spare.

Woodbury Hill (the 'Greenhill' of Hardy's appellation) east of the village is ringed by an Iron Age rampart, within which from the Middle Ages until the early twentieth century was held an annual fair of great local importance, which attracted hucksters, mountebanks and traders from as far away as Birmingham, Norwich, and London. To the north are the chalk hills of central Dorset, and Bere lies at their very edge, on a slope that falls to the heathland by a stream.

> . . . *My little Bere dwells on a hill*
> *Under whose feet the silver trout doth swim,*

wrote Thomas Bastard, who became Vicar in 1591. Here Elfrida, the mother of Edward the Martyr, had a house and certainly

7 *Bere Regis Church, the roof*

Bere was a royal demesne at this time. King John visited it at least six times, probably to hunt.

In 1269-70 half the manor was granted to the Abbey of Tarrant, the other half to the Turbervile family, who acquired the whole after the Dissolution. Yet the Turberviles were Catholics. One of them, who was Bishop of Exeter in the reign of Bloody Mary, lost his see for refusing to take the Oath of Supremacy on the accession of Elizabeth. Other Turberviles settled at Wool and Winterborne Whitchurch, but though the Bere Regis branch was the family's main stem, nothing of them remains here but the tombs in the church, where a man with a headache grimaces at them from a late twelfth-century capital.

The Vicar quoted in the last paragraph was born in Blandford in 1566, of a family whose later members practised architecture with success. His grandfather was probably a blacksmith, but he nevertheless was educated at Winchester and New College, Oxford, where he gained a Perpetual Fellowship in 1588. Three years later he had to relinquish it, apparently for writing scurrilous or, at any rate, offensive verses, and after a short spell as chaplain to Thomas Howard, later Earl of Suffolk, came to Bere. He was married three times, but never wealthily, and he died poor. His satirical poems are worth reading, and Anthony à Wood says of him that 'he was good company to the end, always ready to versify upon any subject'. Alas, poor Yorick. His mind gave way finally, and he died in 1618, having been lodged in prison for debt.

South-west of Bere, on the banks of the Piddle, is a trio of small villages, one on the north, the others on the south bank of the clear and cheerful little stream which brings the alkaline alluvium, like its big sister the Frome, from the central chalk *massif* to neutralise the acid heath soils in its valley. Of these villages, the easternmost, Turnerspuddle is little more than a hamlet with an old church of which only the chancel is now used. The second village, Briantspuddle, has no church, but a fair number of modern houses done up with thatch, the result of a substantial enterprise by Sir Ernest Debenham in the 'thirties. Affpuddle, the third of the triplets, is the solidest, with some cottages of cobb and thatch and a church to whose grey Dorset ashlar and flint is added a golden crown of Ham Hill stone in the form of pinnacles and crenellations on the Perpendicular tower. On the north side of the carefully tended churchyard the Piddle tumbles. The earliest work in the church dates from the mid-thirteenth century, and the pulpit and carved pew-ends were set up in 1547 in the incumbency of Thomas Lylynton, a monk of Cerne Abbey. Appointed vicar in 1534, he kept his place after the Dissolution, his conscience like that of so many clergy at the time permitting him to accept the new order.

The Manor, which had also been the property of Cerne Abbey, came in 1546 to one Oliver Lawrence, quondam Collector of Customs in Poole, member of Parliament for Melcombe Regis in 1529 and for Poole in 1542. One of the Lawrences, who originated in Lancashire, had married an heiress of the Washington family in 1381. For this reason their coat of arms was quartered with that of Washington (three red stars over two stripes) which is supposed to have provided the idea which gave rise to the national flag of the United States. The arms are to be seen on the memorial to Edward Lawrence in the chancel of the church. They are also found in profusion in the church at Steeple, once another Lawrence seat, in Purbeck.

An expanse of heathland south of the Piddle undulates for miles, uninterrupted except by the Frome valley and plantations of conifers, and is scoured by the destructive tanks of the Royal Armoured Corps, whose headquarters at Bovington house the regimental museum. Oddly enough some of the roads over the heath in this area are broad, well-surfaced, and straight, but have no classification by the Ministry of Transport. From some points on them can be seen enormous conical hollows, known as swallet holes, or swallow holes, which used to occasion all kinds of wild surmise among scholars speculating on their origin. Ancient Britons, (especially Druids) and Romans were the most frequent ascriptions. Nowadays they are explained as the result of the washing away by water seepage of chalk underlying the Bagshot beds which form the heathland. The ground surface subsides into the cavity so formed, creating these spectacular pits. The most famous, called Culpepper's Dish, allegedly after the famous herbalist, lies just south of Briantspuddle, has a full-grown oak tree standing in its bottom, but not reaching the level of the rim, and measures a hundred yards across.

In the heart of the heath, half-way between Briantspuddle and Bovington, is Lawrence of Arabia's cottage at Clouds Hill. A high, dense rhododendron hedge hides it from the road, and it stands in a green pool of solitude, enclosed by rhododendron, broom, and oak trees. The National Trust have it now, and keep it furnished much as Lawrence left it. He first rented it when he was stationed as a private at Bovington in 1923, and with the help of a friend made it fit to live in. In 1925 he bought it, using it only as a holiday home, until he left the R.A.F. in 1935, when he began to live permanently in it. Two months later came the motor-cycling accident which killed him.

He called it an earthly paradise, and today it still has the mark of an immensely strong personality. Obviously, he liked leather. A large leather-covered divan dominates the so-called 'book-room' downstairs, and the music room above contains a settee and chair with leather upholstery, while a leather cover and draught excluder obliterate the door. His gramophone with a huge amplifier horn stands in one corner, and on the mantelpiece is a fine bronze head of Lawrence by Kennington. The third living-room, the 'eating room', is quite macabre. Lawrence had it lined with aluminium foil over asbestos as a heat insulator, which produces a peculiarly aseptic and depersonalised effect, despite the picture on the wall, the ship's bunk, and the glass domes under which he kept his food. The cottage still lacks electric light, so that the sense of remoteness, of withdrawal from the twentieth century, is even more marked now than it must have been in 1935. Lawrence is buried in the churchyard at Moreton, a brick and thatch village on the far bank of the Frome, where it meanders through a flat, featureless landscape. The grey stone church, eighteenth-century gothic, built in 1777, was damaged by a bomb in 1940, and benefited in restoration by the insertion in the apsidal east end of five sparkling panels of engraved glass by Lawrence Whistler.

Following the Frome eastward, back towards Wareham, one reaches the dull, suburban-type approaches to Wool, a junction of roads in a land of streams. The old bridge across the river, grey stone with great splashes of pastel-green lichen, has fortunately been relieved of most of the modern traffic, though it still carries a narrow road. At its northern end is the manor house, once a Turbervile seat, and now a hotel, but still very Jacobean with its tall, fluted chimney stacks and stone-mullioned windows, its grey stone south face, and its courtyard of warm red brick to the north. It is the house of Tess's ghastly honeymoon, and eastward (further away than Hardy places it) is the site of an associated incident in the novel, Bindon Abbey. Here the stone coffin in which the sleepwalking Angel Clare placed his wife is still set in the ground in the Abbey ruins, a strangely moving thing by its association with a great work of art. In their present condition, crumbling, or quite crumbled, with low remnants of wall in red stone hung with creepers and rock-plants, and the immense bases of great piers that once supported the nave of the church now bare and isolated, the ruins are a delight to the romantic imagination. The fish ponds still remain, bordered by walks in cloister-like avenues of smooth-boled beeches.

The Cistercian Abbey was originally founded at Little Bindon, near Lulworth, in 1149 and kept its name when it was enlarged and moved to Wool by the local lord, Robert de Newburgh, and his wife Matilda, in 1172. After the Dissolution it was demolished, and some of its stones were used for building Portland and Sandsfoot Castles. It was plundered again later in the century for Lulworth Castle, and many cottages in the older part of Wool itself incorporate material filched from the labours of the monks.

The main road through Wool, the principal route from Dorchester, returns to Wareham on the east to exemplify the town's position as gateway to and from the river valleys. The road south displays it as gateway to the Isle of Purbeck, which is no island at all geographically. Purbeck is bordered on the north by the Frome and Poole Harbour, on the east and south by the sea. Its western boundary is the little stream called Luckford Lake, which placidly joins the Frome near East Stoke, having flowed over the southern heath from the area of East Lulworth. Purbeck is even less of an island, then, than Thanet, which was once separated from the mainland by a wide channel, as Purbeck never has been. Yet, because it lay on no great routes, and had no centres of great military or economic importance, it echoes in exaggerated form the history and condition of the whole county, and possesses true insularity in landscape and character. Its northern part is heath, over which towers a long lofty green ridge of chalk running from Studland to Worbarrow, from sea to sea, rising in places to over 600 feet, but rarely more than half a mile wide. The views from the top are often breathtaking, most of them accessible only on foot, but once there the eye may travel over the brown heath and the blue sea, over the valley that forms the heart of Purbeck, over the distant inlets and islands of Poole Harbour, all laid out like a carpet. The ridgeway along it is rich in barrows (there is a notable group on Nine Barrow Down) and at the point where it meets the sea above Worbarrow Bay is an Iron Age camp, Flowers Barrow, unique in its kind by virtue of its situation on a cliff edge, and half devoured by the sea. The only true gap in the chalk is at Corfe Castle, where the Corfe River and a tributary have isolated a great knoll on which the castle stands, though at Ulwell the road from Studland to Swanage crosses by a saddle between Ballard Down and Godlingston Hill.

South of the chalk a long valley of Wealden clay runs from Swanage to Worbarrow, a mile or so wide all the way, then beyond that is the coastal mass of oolitic limestone and Kimmeridge clay, rising less steeply out of the valley than the chalk, but dropping sharply to the south and ending in abrupt, rugged cliffs at the sea's edge.

The northern heath is wide, flat, and often marshy. Indeed the road from Wareham as far as Stoborough (which until 1714 had its own manor) is a causeway over ground often waterlogged. To the east and west the land is sour and wild, marked in places by clay workings, for this was and largely still is the provenance of the fine clay on which the nineteenth-century prosperity of Poole was founded. On or near the harbour shore the only settlement of any significance at all today is the hamlet of Arne, at the end of three miles of road through heather and gorse. Built on a fertile patch by a knoll, it consists of a farmhouse and a few cottages, and a simple thirteenth-century chapel of brown rubble and grey ashlar. Ower, further east, was one of the points from which clay was shipped to Poole, and in the Middle Ages flourished as the port for the Purbeck marble quarried at Worth Matravers. There is now no public road to it, and it survives as a single house. Further east still is the place called Newton where, in the time of Edward I men built a new town indeed, for a port (which indicates the significance of Purbeck stone in medieval times). It came to nothing and disappeared shortly after its founding, perhaps because of the ever-encroaching silt that was also choking the trade of Wareham.

To the west of Stoborough two roads run south. One of them leads past Furzebrook, and the Blue Pool to which holiday-makers come by coach-loads in the summer. The attraction is the colour of the water in a wide, disused clay pit, whose creamy cliffs, veined with harder, pink rock, are draped with bushes and overhung with pine trees. The water is a rich, deep turquoise because of the suspension in it of minute particles of clay, and in fact outdoes even the picture postcards on sale in the inevitable kiosk.

The other road (the first turning from Wareham) leads to Creech Grange, a partly Elizabethan house with additions in the eighteenth and nineteenth centuries. It stands in finely landscaped grounds, with lakes, peacocks, and woodland paths set under the great mound of Creech Barrow and the sheer green wall of Ridgeway Hill, which is clothed on its northern slope with a dense mantle of trees. Deer may be seen even at the top of the hill, reminding us that Purbeck was once a royal forest. At the northern edge of the wood on the very summit of the hill stands an eighteenth-century gateway to nowhere, erected for the sake of the view from Creech Grange.

Corfe Castle itself, strategically placed to command the only route through the hills, is the centre of Purbeck, its gaunt ruins still towering over the village like skeletal warning fingers. Its history is violent and it came to a poor end, but so spectacular, so evocative are the stones that remain, the crumbling wreck of the keep, the crazily tilted watch towers, the square, forceful silhouette like a sculpture of an Aztec god on a heroic skyline, that it has become almost monotonously familiar through picture postcards, calendars and table mats. Somehow its dignity has survived. Its great natural mound, lower than the hills to east and west, was none the less high enough before the invention of guns to control the way into southern Purbeck. When it was first fortified we do not know, but it is first mentioned in 978 in connection with the murder of Edward the Martyr, whose stepmother, Elfrida, had a house or hunting lodge at Corfe, perhaps on the site of the castle. Anxious to secure the succession of her own son, Ethelred, known later as 'the Unready', she had Edward killed by one of her attendants when he had come to visit her there. The king, on horseback, called for wine and received the fatal blow as he raised his drink to his mouth.

8   *Corfe Castle, the ruined keep*

9 (above) *Cerne Abbas, looking over the village, showing the Giant and Church*

10 (below) *Arne Heath*

According to one version, indeed, Elfrida herself stabbed him. In agony he rode off, but fainted. His feet catching in the stirrup as he fell, his horse dragged him horribly some distance over the rough ground until it stopped, and the king was dead. He was buried first in Wareham (the church of Lady St. Mary still has his reputed coffin), and three years later exhumed and 'still uncorrupted' taken to Shaftesbury. Tradition says that when Elfrida, who had retired to Bere Regis, tried in contrition to follow his second funeral, her horse could not be prevented from backing away, so that she dismounted and tried to follow on foot, only to discover herself also miraculously unable to walk in the procession. She subsequently founded nunneries at Amesbury and at Whorwell, Hampshire, where she died.

The castle existed by the reign of Stephen, when Baldwin de Redvers seized it for Matilda, and 60 years later John used it as a prison for state captives, and a repository for his regalia. After the murder of his nephew Arthur, John lodged Eleanor, the prince's sister, in Corfe, where she stayed until the king's death. She was then removed to Bristol until her own, which ended 40 years in captivity. In 1209 she had been joined by two daughters of the king of Scotland, handed over as hostages. The three women were well treated and allowed some luxuries, but of 24 knights taken at the same time as Eleanor and sent to Corfe all but two were allowed to die of starvation. In the same reign one, Peter of Pomfret, who rashly predicted in 1212 that the king would lose his throne before the next Ascension Day, on being proved wrong, was dragged by horses from Corfe Castle to Wareham and back, then hanged and quartered with his son. In 1326 Edward II stayed briefly in the Castle, a prisoner, in the custody of Matravers and Gurney, who later murdered him at Berkely. His brother, Edmund, Earl of Kent, was deliberately given reason to think that Edward was still alive at Corfe. Messengers he sent to the Constable, who was a henchman of Queen Isabella and her paramour, Mortimer, reported (had they been bribed, or deceived?) that they had seen the king and that a

11 *Lulworth Castle*

letter from Kent would be given to him. Of course, it went to Mortimer instead, and Kent was executed for treason.

The Constable of Corfe Castle, a royal appointee, had considerable importance at this time in Purbeck, not merely as custodian of the only Royal castle in Dorset, and commander of the king's garrison, but as civil representative of the central government. Although Henry III disafforested Purbeck, it remained a royal warren, and the Constable had to enforce the strict regulations relating to commerce and land use that always accompanied royal or aristocratic hunting rights. Indeed, so close was the control over the inhabitants that no Purbeck woman could marry a man from outside the island except with the permission of the Constable. Even as late as the reign of Elizabeth the islanders could not be summoned to Petty Sessions outside Purbeck, and were immune from arrest by the Sheriff of Dorset without the approval of the Mayor of Corfe Castle.

Queen Elizabeth granted Corfe Castle (with the office of Vice Admiral of Purbeck) to Sir Christopher Hatton, who left it to his nephew, Sir William Hatton, through whom it came to his widow, Lady Elizabeth. She was a woman of fiery temperament who, refusing an offer of marriage to Lord Bacon, became the wife of his enemy, Sir Edward Coke. Her spectacular domestic rows were a public scandal for years. Perhaps their culmination was her kidnapping of her own daughter to prevent her marrying Sir John Villiers, brother of the Duke of Buckingham, and the girl's recapture by Coke by main force. The daughter's marriage, one need hardly add, in the circumstances, was as unhappy as her mother's and equally stormy. On Coke's death, his widow and daughter sold Corfe Castle to Sir John Bankes, with whose purchase the final stage in its history began.

Bankes settled his family in the castle after 1634, and in 1642 in his absence with the King at York his wife put it into a condition to withstand attack. This came indeed in early 1643, when a force under Sir Walter Erle came from Poole to demand sub-mission. The gates were shut just in time to prevent the entrance of a party of horsemen by a stratagem, and Lady Bankes sat firm, though with the minutest possible garrison, which had to be reinforced by the womenfolk. To a summons to surrender her ordnance ('four small pieces') she replied by firing one of them, and generally acquitted herself pretty well. Nevertheless the Parliamentarians invested the castle closely, so that she finally handed over her artillery on condition that the castle should not be molested. The breathing space she had won she used by gathering arms, stores, and extra manpower, including men from the army of Prince Maurice at Blandford, who also sent her Captain Edward Lawrence to command the enlarged garrison. She must have had every intention, when she gave up her guns, of ensuring that the castle would indeed be molested.

It was. A force bombarded it from the hills, but the artillery of the day was not powerful enough to make much impression. On June 20, 1643, Erle occupied the town but failed to take the castle in six weeks of vain attacks, for the purposes of which he used the church as a vantage point for artillery, and melted down the organ-pipes to make musket balls. At last, on hearing of the approach of a relief force, he withdrew to Poole by sea from Wareham. At this time the Royalists had the upper hand in Dorset, and had taken Wareham, Dorchester, and Weymouth, all of which had declared for Parliament at the very beginning of the war. Only Poole and Lyme Regis held out against them. Corfe Castle, therefore, remained inviolate until 1645, when a blockade was begun under the orders of Sir Anthony Ashley-Cooper. Again, Lady Bankes refused to surrender, but events elsewhere were against her. No Prince Maurice appeared to help her, for no other Royalist garrison remained between London and Exeter. She held on nevertheless until at length a certain Col. Pitman agreed to betray the castle in return for a safe conduct. Leaving on the pretext of fetching reinforcements from Somerset, he came back with a hundred men who in fact were

Roundheads from Weymouth. By pre-arrangement, as soon as his party was inside, the besiegers attacked, and surrender was inevitable.

Parliament decided to 'slight' the castle, that is, to destroy it, and engineers toiled hard to carry out that decision. Ruin it they certainly did, but their seventeenth-century explosives were not powerful enough to obliterate it, so that we can still admire the work of those medieval builders whose masonry withstood their efforts. The village, so dominated by the great fortress that it has taken its name, though it is sometimes called simply 'Corfe' for short, is entirely of grey stone cottages and houses with stone roofs, and would be worth a visit on its own account, even without its heirloom on the hill-top. Many of the buildings date from the eighteenth century, and some, notably the diminutive town hall that serves as a museum, from the seventeenth.

Just north of the castle, a road runs eastward, winding alternately through heath and woodland, to the seaside hamlet of Studland. Incidentally it passes, near Rempstone Hall, one of Dorset's prehistoric stone circles set surprisingly in the heath at the foot of Nine Barrow Down and therefore a curio. It has stood there, a frozen ballet in brown heath stone, since early in the Bronze Age. The bay at Studland looks east to the Isle of Wight, with the suburban smear of Bournemouth and Poole clearly to be seen to the north-east. A peninsula of sand runs northward to divide Poole Harbour from the sea—not a narrow line like the Sandbanks peninsula on the north of the harbour mouth, but a broad-based formation a mile wide at the south and narrowing quite gradually to South Haven Point, from which a car-ferry plies to Sandbanks. By the sea this sand is flat and smooth, and vastly popular in the summer, giving way some distance from the water's edge to dunes covered with marram grass. In its heart the peninsula is sour, like the Great Heath, but the gorse and heather and much rarer flora which flourish here enwrap astonishingly a lake, the Little Sea, whose shores are a Nature Reserve.

At Studland a red cliff introduces like a grace note the first of the rockier splendours of the Dorset coast, where the edge of the land, consisting of chalk after a short distance, turns sharply eastward to Handfast Point and the Old Harry Rocks. The village is characterless, but redeemed by the only virtually complete Norman church in Dorset, a squat-towered, pale grey blockhouse of a building, an utterly functional exterior, except for the stone grotesques under the eaves of the nave, set in a churchyard of contrasting lushness. The dark interior, lit in Norman fashion by few windows, has a most powerful simplicity which the minor alterations of later centuries (such as the Early English east window, and the eighteenth-century gallery) have not effaced.

Among the tombstones in the churchyard is one on the grave of Sgt. William Lawrence, of the 40th Regiment of Foot, who was born in Briantspuddle in 1790. He was apprenticed in 1804 to a Studland builder, who ill treated him, and from whom he ran away and joined the army. He fought in South America, in the Peninsular War (he was wounded at Badajoz) and at Waterloo, and he brought back what must have been a rare curiosity at the time in a remote Dorset village, a French wife. They ran a public house together at Studland after his discharge and died, she in 1853, he in 1869. Lawrence left an autobiography of great interest dictated, since he was illiterate, to a friend after the death of his Clotilde. He represents himself as a man of courage and humanity, something of a bravo in his youth, even a firebrand, but resourceful and ready for all eventualities.

The cliffs between Studland and Swanage, forming the end of the chalk ridge, are groined by the sea into caverns and miniature bays between great buttresses of chalk, which in places have been isolated from the parent rock and stand unsupported, waiting for destruction. The sea washes the entire length of coast even at low tide, but crossing the hills on foot offers splendours which more than compensate for the inaccessibility of the base of the cliffs. Swanage, the largest settlement, the only town in Purbeck, is a dreadful anticlimax. It lies on the Wealden clay between the chalk and the oolite in a bay of scenic drama. To the north is Ballard Point, and the chalk wall of Ballard Cliff, streaked with green where plant life clings to crumbling ledges, and Ballard Down, whose smooth undulations lead the eye westward and inland. On the south are Peveril Point, and cliffs of contorted limestone, with fingers of rock probing the sea just below its surface. Perhaps these are the very reefs on which the Viking fleet of 120 ships met its destruction at the hands of the weather and Alfred the Great in 877. The sea wall and the sandy beach curl from Ballard Cliff to Peveril Point, protecting a grey Victorian seaside town where most of the interesting things have a touch of the ludicrous. What can we make of a memorial to Alfred's victory crowned by cannon-balls captured in the Crimea? Or a clock-tower without a clock, once a memorial to the Duke of Wellington at the Southwark end of London Bridge? Or a town-hall with a facade (said to be by Wren) lifted from the Mercers' Hall in Cheapside? These wonders were the gifts to their native town of two quarrymen, who made fortunes in stone in London, and one of whom placed near Durlston Head, to the south, a monstrous piece of Portland stone carved into a terrestrial globe, and set it about with sententious quotations. Before these men charity and civic pride had donated a minute stone lock-up, about eight feet by ten, ventilated only through holes bored in the door, and bearing the message, 'Erected for the prevention of vice and immorality by the Friends of Religion and Good Order. 1803'.

On the credit side, there is a good row of Victorian shops on the front, near the Square, cheerfully detailed and coloured. The Public Library is an excellent twelve-sided modern building of the mid-sixties in steel, glass and Purbeck stone, with a decidedly friendly interior. There are several good Georgian pubs, and one or two odd little back entries, and a few old (with some less old) houses by the Mill Pond, which will disappoint anyone whose expectations are based on the flattering publicity photographs.

Historically Swanage and the Purbeck stone industry are inextricably linked. Four main types of building stone have been quarried in the Isle of Purbeck for many centuries. The most important is the one called Portland stone, named appropriately enough after the area in which the most abundant supplies are found. Stone from the Middle Purbeck formation is used for paving, roofing, and kerbing, as well as building, while from the rocks of the Upper Purbeck are obtained the 'burr', which is a coarser limestone, and the better known Purbeck marble. This is not a true marble, but a limestone crowded with the shells of a freshwater snail. It is found in various colours—green, buff, and reddish brown—and can take a high polish. It was popular in the Middle Ages, when it was used in the building of churches and cathedrals (for instance, Canterbury, Winchester, and Salisbury) and again in the Gothic revival among the Victorians. The Romans used it when they first occupied Britain, for broken slabs have been found at Colchester in rubbish pits dated to A.D. 61, but as they discovered that it weathers rapidly out of doors, they became less enthusiastic.

To the west of Swanage the hills of southern Purbeck near Langton Matravers and Worth Matravers are scarred with quarry workings, like the fulfilment of a curse. The Tilly Whim caves to the south, near Durlston Head, are disused cliff-side quarries, from which the cut blocks of stone were loaded direct into boats for transport to Swanage, where they were transshipped. At Winspit, near Worth Matravers, is the largest and oldest cliff-side quarry in Purbeck (now disused), where the stone had to be lowered as much as 30 feet into barges. Swanage seems to have become the port for Purbeck stone as Ower silted up. In the eighteenth century and earlier the shore of Swanage Bay was broken by stone quays about three feet high, called 'bankers', to which men carried stone actually on their backs for loading into boats, which in their turn took it to the freight vessels waiting off shore. It was only on the arrival of the railway as late as 1887 that the bankers were disused and demolished.

Like most of Swanage itself, the Purbeck villages are built of the plentiful local stone, so that all Purbeck from Lulworth to Ballard Point has become a study in grey and green, especially as the large fields on the hills are divided by drystone walls instead of hedges and fences. The villages are all set back from the savage coast, in sheltered positions, so that one may walk along the cliff top from Swanage westwards as far as the beginning of the Army's ranges beyond Kimmeridge Bay uninterrupted by the work of men, apart from an occasional stile. Here and there, for instance, at Dancing Ledge, Winspit, Chapman's Pool, and Kimmeridge Bay, one can descend to the water's edge, though not always without difficulty, but most of the way one is well above sea level, as hill-top, bay, and cliff interweave in a slow visual polyphony.

Worth Matravers lies a mile inland from Winspit, and is by far the most interesting of the villages south of Corfe. It has a charming village pond, a church whose Norman chancel arch bears elaborate chevron ornamentation, and the grave of Benjamin Jesty, whose tombstone claims him as the discoverer of vaccination, 20 years before Jenner. He is said 'from his great strength of mind' to have tried this desperate prophylactic on his wife and sons, but must have decided that his own health was too valuable to risk. Winspit lies on the south-east side of the great foreland of St. Aldhelm's Head, which rises almost sheer out of the sea to a height of over 350 feet. On its summit stands a tiny but very solid twelfth-century chapel, which is still used. At one time it probably bore a cresset on its roof instead of the modern cross now there, and served as landmark and warning for sailors. Next to it is the coastguard station, painted in a phosphorescent orange which however functional it may be destroys any sense of remoteness. We are firmly in the twentieth century.

On the other side of the Head, where the Portland stone is overlaid with black, crumbling Kimmeridge clay, the sea has scooped out a bay floored with greyish sand, where the indiscriminating bathe. Here nature dwarfs and domineers, St. Aldhelm's on one side rearing up like a fortress on a green mountain, on the other Hounstout Cliff, shaped like a gigantic cottage loaf from which a slice has been hacked. A rough path (not recommended for the elderly) leads down from a place where cars may be parked, if their owners will tolerate the rock-strewn surface of the track which leads to it from the village of Kingston. This little grey stone place has two churches, one in use, designed by Street and much admired by some, the other, locked and disused, built by Lord Eldon, Pitt's Lord Chancellor, who lived in the neighbouring valley of Encombe.

The son of a trader of Newcastle-on-Tyne, named Scott, and a man of obviously high ability, Eldon was yet one of English history's less attractive characters, an illiberal reactionary, who resisted Catholic emancipation and the repeal of the Test Act, defended the notorious Six Acts of 1819, and, predictably, opposed the Reform Bill in 1832. 'His last speech in Parliament', say Hutchins' editors, 'seems to have been against the "dangerous innovation" of the Great Western Railway'. He died in 1838 and is buried at Kingston.

Two miles further west is Kimmeridge, which gives its name to the shaly clay which outcrops here. The village is neat and tidy, rather than picturesque, but the coastal scenery nearly compensates for that. The black cliffs are low, and the undercliff, on which a thin drizzle of tiny clay fragments rains, is strewn with scraps of shale and limestone, a band of which about two feet thick runs in the cliff all around the bay. Flat ledges of this limestone stretch out into the sea, a particularly broad one on the western side of the bay being appropriately called 'The Flats'.

In the clay lies a band about 34 inches thick of a black oil shale known as Kimmeridge coal, because it burns, though with a sulphurous smell. Freshly quarried, it is hard and may be polished. In several places near Kimmeridge finds have been made of discs of this substance, to the puzzlement of early antiquaries, who decided that they were used as coins, and called them 'coal money'. To explain it they concocted an elaborate story to the effect that the Phoenicians had settled here with a view to making pottery from Kimmeridge clay, using oil shale as a fuel for firing their products. The 'coal money' was supposed to have been made as a thank-offering to Hercules for their prosperity. The truth is more interesting. In Iron Age times the shale was used for the manufacture of armlets, which were produced on a lathe. The cores were abandoned on the working sites, to be discovered and misinterpreted by eighteenth-century gentlemen. The industry continued into Roman times on a large scale, but died out after the fourth century. The Romans also used the shale for making trays and furniture, pieces of which may be seen in the county museum in Dorchester.

The neighbouring country house of Smedmore (often open to the public) stands in a short valley, with a green slope to the north, and a swelling of the land to protect it from the sea to the south. Outwardly it is of the eighteenth century, its west front, which the visitor encounters first, furnished with two great bows like semicircular buttresses, which give it an air of solidity and good sense. On the far side are traces of the Jacobean building which is the core of the house, a little yard with a stone-mullioned window of the seventeenth century, and a Tudor Gothic doorway leading into the garden, itself a delight. Inside, the house has some eighteenth-century plasterwork, an oak staircase with balusters of alternating patterns, and the quiet assurance shared with, for instance, St. Giles and Winterborne Clenston, that seems to belong with ownership by one family for centuries.

The estate of Smedmore last changed hands by purchase in

1391, but the Jacobean house is more recent, being built by Sir William Clavell, who lived originally in the partly thirteenth-century house at Barnston, near Church Knowle. He moved, one imagines, to be near the alum works he established at Kimmeridge. However comfortable the house, the alum proved disastrous, since a monopoly was granted to competitors, and Clavell forced to stop his operations, which cost him £2,000. Nothing daunted, he launched into making glass, using the oily shale as fuel, but again ran foul of monopolists, spent some time in the Marshalsea, and ended his life with debts which it took three generations to pay off. Other commercial attempts to exploit Kimmeridge coal have proved unsuccessful, if not as catastrophic as Sir William's.

Both an advantage and a source of bitter exasperation to living in Purbeck, or visiting it, is the difficulty of ingress and therefore of egress. Virtually there is only one way in and out, that through Wareham, which figures regularly in the news bulletins during the holiday months as the site of almost unspeakable traffic jams. A detour on the way out can be made at Stoborough, via West Holme, but this leads westward and is of limited value to those who want the Bournemouth or Poole routes. Access from the west would be easier if the military did not occupy the coast, the Wealden valley, the chalk ridge, and the heath to the west of Steeple and Kimmeridge. Sometimes the roads here are open and when they are they are worth taking.

The road from East Lulworth to Steeple (and it is best travelled from west to east) is the most thrilling in Dorset. The fields on either side are wired off and the route punctuated by ferocious warnings, like drumbeats, against straying from the road for fear of unexploded shells. But one climbs and climbs up White-way Hill, and the heathland spreads out on the north like the floor of the world, while the hill rises everlastingly higher to the south. After tantalisingly skirting the summit, with a sudden shift seawards the road marches along the crest of the chalk ridge as though on a knife edge for a mile and a quarter of splendour. There are several parking places, but a large one has been thoughtfully provided overlooking the Purbeck valley, with the ruined village of Tyneham in the middle distance, Flowers Barrow and its ramparts prominent on the right and Portland, low and menacing, behind it.

In August, and only rarely at other times, the road to Tyneham is open. The village and its Elizabethan manor house were alive in 1939, but occupied during the war with the unfulfilled promise that it would be returned to its owners after the emergency. One parks one's car in a field, and walks for a mile to the coast at Worbarrow Bay, where the sea cuts through the valley and the hills to expose their geology like a layer cake on its side. The limestone juts into the sea in the little peninsula called Worbarrow Tout, which on its eastern side forms one arm of Pondfield Cove, an inlet with cliffs of grey and creamy limestone in sharply tilted strata, and pools crowded with sea anemones. Westward comes a half-mile of Wealden beds—clays, sands, and marls of reds, oranges, browns, and greys, like a mass of creeper in autumn on a grey stone wall. This variegated display is followed by the chalk cliff of Rings Hill, marbled with lines and streaks of living green, and crowned by Flowers Barrow camp, which is inaccessible because of unexploded shells. Beyond is the little inlet of Arish Mell, once a haunt of smugglers, then more chalk cliffs, and the reappearance of the oolite in Mupe Bay and the Mupe Rocks, which stand in the same relation to Worbarrow Tout as Old Harry to the Needles. Round the corner, invisible from Worbarrow, is Lulworth Cove and the glittering coastline beyond it, but to reach it we must return inland from Tyneham and go back over Whiteway Hill, then through East Lulworth.

Near this village in a large walled park stands the ruin of Lulworth Castle, which was gutted by fire in 1929. Its building was begun in 1588 by Henry, the second Lord Howard of Bindon, not as a fortress, of course, but as a residence. He was a wild and eccentric character, a man of violence who associated as accomplice and drinking companion with pirates and smugglers, and caused his father, the first Viscount, a good deal of trouble. At one stage he put away his wife and child and took a mistress, he beat his wife, who had to seek her father-in-law's protection, and actually spent a month in the Marshalsea for his outrageous behaviour. A commission of the Privy Council, investigating a claim he made on some of his father's lands reported that he was not to be trusted with firearms, and we have a record of an encounter between Henry Howard and several local dignitaries near Wimborne, when he assaulted one of them, Thomas Chafin of Folke, by knocking off his hat, pulling his beard, and offering him other indignities. In the end Queen Elizabeth herself intervened in his private life, so scandalous had it become. His daughter married secretly, but in the presence of her mother, a man of whom Lord Bindon disapproved (he had just succeeded to the title). When he learned of the match, he so frenziedly maltreated his wretched wife, a former lady-in-waiting to the Queen, that Elizabeth had her removed from his home. Reluctantly he let her go, her party taking only his very meanest horses, but accompanied by the richest vituperation.

Two years after beginning his castle he died, to be succeeded by his brother, Thomas, whom Sir Walter Raleigh described as 'a peevish fool'. He sold the estate, about 1605, to the Earl of Suffolk, who finished the castle in 1609. In 1641 it was again sold, to Humphrey Weld, a member of an old Catholic family, whose descendants still own and occupy it. During the Civil War it was seized by Parliamentary forces, who stripped it of lead and iron for use by Roundheads in Poole and Weymouth, and at the siege of Corfe Castle. It was visited in 1665 by Charles II, and later by James II. More interestingly, George III and his family were entertained here several times during their various sojournings in Weymouth, and Lulworth was for a time the home of the future Mrs. Fitzherbert, who as Mary Ann Smythe had married Edward Weld, only to be widowed at the age of 18 in the following year. We are told that Thomas Weld had meals for his royal guests (the King and Queen and their six children) 'served upon entirely new services of gold and silver, on every piece of which was engraved, "Long Live the King"'.

What we are not told is whether George ever became tired of the reiteration of this sentiment by his loyal Dorset subjects. In Weymouth, when they went out to walk, the royal family were greeted by crowds shouting it, varied to 'God save the King', children wore hats, sailors cockades, and the bathing machine women girdles all bearing the same legend. It was painted on the machines themselves, and on every house in the town. When the King took his first bathe, a band of fiddlers in a neighbouring machine played the anthem fervently as the waters of the Channel enveloped the royal torso.

A later royal visitor to Lulworth Castle was Charles X of France, who found refuge for some months there after the revolution of 1830. Previously, Sir Robert Peel had the tenancy for some three years. The remains are still impressive, and so complete that it is not until one is relatively close that the hollowness of the grey shell, with large crenellated turrets at each of its four corners, becomes obvious. Certainly, enough is left to make comprehensible Charles X's remark on first seeing it—'Voilà, la Bastille'.

In the grounds, which are sometimes open to the public, is a domed chapel, built by Thomas Weld in 1786, and the first Roman Catholic church to be built in England after the Reformation. A picture gallery is housed in what used to be the stables and contains an interesting collection, of which the cream is a set of four splendid Brussels tapestries of the end of the seventeenth century from cartoons by Teniers. They are full of vitality and interest, in excellent condition (their colours still rich and deep) and displayed to perfection in a room adapted specially for them.

Divided from East Lulworth by the unsightly complex of Lulworth Camp, the village of West Lulworth includes some
pleasant old cottages, and the shore of Lulworth Cove and all
that goes with it. In short, in the summer it is jammed with
traffic and thick with sightseers, a pandemonium of traffic fumes,
transistor radios, far more people than it was built to contain,
a car park almost as big as the Cove itself, an unsightly scatter
of souvenir shops, and a smell of chips. But the holiday industry
has not been allowed to destroy the Cove, which should be
visited out of season. A wall of Portland stone, which to the
east and a little way westward, protects the chalk against
erosion, has suffered a 400 foot breach through which the sea
has battered away the softer rock to make an almost circular
bay. On the north side is the steep chalk cliff of Bindon Hill (in
military occupation) at the foot of which the road leads down
to the shingle beach, where lobster pots remind us that the
holiday industry overlies an older economic base. Immediately
to the west, the sea has begun a fresh breach in the limestone
at Stair Hole which in a few centuries will be linked with Lulworth Cove. Meanwhile, its fantastically contorted strata offer
a vivid illustration of the immense power of the earth move-
ments that laid the foundations of this scenery a hundred million
years ago.

By the coastal path from Lulworth to White Nothe, about four
miles away, even in summer one can find solitude, once past
Durdle Door. Here, a poorly screened caravan camp, which
splashes the sober downs with all the zany and indiscriminate
colouring of modern camping equipment, spills its inhabitants
on to a long, narrow beach. The Door, a huge natural arch of
Portland stone, leans into the mid-day sun because of the sloping
of the strata here, and a narrow isthmus joins it to the mainland
as though supporting it. The cliffs are brilliant, haggard walls of
chalk—to the east Hambury Tout, to the west Swyre Head—
and the path switchbacks along their edge. Further on comes
Bat's Head where the strata are again vertical, studded with

flints like rows of rivets, and there is nothing to see but the gulls in and out of their nests on the cliffs, lines of white foam appearing and dissolving rhythmically below to the beat of the sea on the pebbly shore, and grass and scabious and bee orchids, and the gigantic undulations of downland. At White Nothe, another promontory of chalk and the last cliff of that rock in Dorset, the land has slipped seaward, and the cliff has become a shambles, with slopes, grass-covered ledges, and little vales, very romantic, in contrast with the classical purity and finality of the sheer drop at Swyre Head.

Below White Nothe westward is the modern settlement at Ringstead Bay, on the site of a medieval village said to have been destroyed in a French raid in 1420, when the raiders burnt down the church in which the villagers had taken refuge. Alternatively, it may have been depopulated by the Black Death. The chancel of the church is now a cottage, in whose garden medieval bones are still dug up, and in which a Transitional Norman arch is still to be seen upstairs.

At Osmington Mills, a mile further on, past a radar installation, a little stream cuts its way through Corallian rocks to the sea. Inland, off the Weymouth-Wareham road, the village of Osmington stands, neat, bright and homely. Its grey stone church is largely restored, but contains in the chancel a curious sixteenth-century monument. It has three inscriptions. The first, in Latin reads: 'I have reached harbour. Farewell, hope and fortune —I have no more to do with you. Now sport with other people.' Below this, we read: 'Man's life. Man is a glas. Life is as water thats weakly walld about. Sinne bringes in Death. Death breakes the glas. So runnes the water out. Finis.' Lastly, cut vertically on the edge of the stone is the cryptic legend: 'Here is not the man who in his life with every man had law and strife.' All these inscriptions are cut crudely, the letters ill-formed and most abominably spaced, imperfections which add piquancy to the anonymity of the monument. Since it bears the Warham

12　*Stair Hole, Lulworth*

coat of arms it presumably commemorates a member of that family, but how he managed to introduce such bitter and implicitly non-Christian sentiment into a memorial inside a church we can only imagine. And does the third inscription indicate a late repentance, or is it a macabre joke on a cenotaph?

The Warhams, one of whom as Archbishop of Canterbury in the reigns of Henry VII and Henry VIII, was sketched by Holbein, probably lived in the house whose ruins adjoin the churchyard. Osmington itself was painted by Constable, who spent part of his honeymoon in the vicarage. A large white horse, with a rider, is cut in the turf of White Horse Hill, north of the village. He is steadily plodding away from Weymouth, whose citizens had him made in celebration of King George III's patronage of their municipality. Not far off, by the villages of Poxwell, Warmwell, and Owermoigne respectively, are three old manor houses, Poxwell and Warmwell both of the early seventeenth century, and Owermoigne Court dating back much further. Warmwell, whose garden is occasionally open to the public, is a curiosity in that it was designed as a suntrap, with east and west wings set obliquely to the centre block. Part of Owermoigne Court was built about 1270, and what was the hall (built on first-floor level) retains its Decorated windows and window seats, so that it may claim, with Barnston and Woodsford Castle (four miles to the north) to be one of the three oldest inhabited houses in the county.

Moving back towards Weymouth, one passes at Preston a huge caravan site, unbelievably naked and hideous, but the little church is worth a glance. It has a charming monument to an anonymous (and untraced) vicar of the early seventeenth century, and a twentieth-century window with delicately coloured glass reminiscent of book illustrations by Dulac or Rackham.

Of Weymouth itself much is today a regrettable sprawl along a ruined coast and hinterland. Bowleaze Cove, for instance, which

13 *Weymouth Harbour, a popular mooring for yachtsmen*

Constable painted, boasts a holiday camp, caravans, bingo, and other appurtenances of modern mass leisure. The approach from Dorchester is dull with the dullness of the 1930's. The distinguished church of Wyke Regis (the mother-church of Weymouth) and its huge cemetery in which lie the remains of scores of victims of shipwreck on Chesil Bank, stands on a knoll surrounded by a sea of mediocrity. Despite these and other disappointments, Weymouth at its core, along its Esplanade, and round its harbour, where the Radipole Lake empties into the sea, has a vitality that some other seaside resorts should envy.

The modern borough is the result of a fusion of two old ones —Weymouth itself, on the south side of the harbour, and Melcombe Regis on the north. Weymouth is mentioned in a Saxon charter of the reign of Athelstan, but in the neighbourhood traces of Roman occupation have been found—at Jordan Hill, near Preston, and at Radipole, which was the port for Maiden Castle. Even older is the Iron Age fort at Chalbury. The manor of Weymouth, with those of Portland, Wyke Regis, and Elwell, was given by Edward the Confessor to St. Swithin's, Winchester, to atone for the false accusation against his mother of immoral association with Alwyn, Bishop of Winchester. She had proved her innocence, according to the story by walking 'blindfold and barefoot over nine ploughshares of red-hot iron'. Weymouth passed out of the hands of the Church, for it formed part of the dowry of Eleanor of Castile, Queen of Edward I, from which time it began to prosper. In 1347 it supplied ships and sailors for the siege of Calais, but in 1377 suffered a destructive raid by the French. In 1471 Margaret of Anjou landed there to begin the disastrous campaign which ended with the Lancastrian defeat at Tewkesbury.

Meanwhile, Melcombe (where the Black Death entered England in 1348) was flourishing also. The manor had belonged to Cerne Abbey, but like Weymouth formed part of Queen Eleanor's dowry. In 1280 Edward I granted it a charter with apparently exceptional privileges, which formed a model for those later granted to Poole and Lyme. It became a staple town under Edward III. Late in the fourteenth century, however, French raids seem to have seriously diminished its prosperity, which lapsed again after a revival under Edward IV.

In the reign of Elizabeth the two boroughs, after years of bickering particularly over harbour dues and revenues, were united administratively and at the end of the century the union was consummated with the building of a bridge over the water between them, the very ancestor of the one which stands today. Communication previously had been by ferry. Nowadays Melcombe is a name hardly mentioned, yet most of the usual holiday attractions are in what was that borough. The main shopping centre, the railway and bus stations, places of entertainment, and the long curve of the Esplanade, none of these is in old Weymouth, which is a hugger-mugger of narrow streets and nineteenth-century buildings. By the harbour are, however, several good groups of bow-fronted Georgian houses, and some pretty harbourscapes, as sailing craft at anchor make patterns with their masts and rigging.

On the outbreak of the Civil War the united boroughs like the other Dorset ports declared for Parliament, only to fall to the King in 1643. In the following year the Earl of Essex re-took Weymouth from the Royalists, though in 1645 they all but recaptured it. After the Civil War the port declined, the harbour silted up, and Poole rose on the Newfoundland trade. It was the new fashion of sea bathing which revived Weymouth's fortunes in the eighteenth century. The first bathing machines were established in 1748 on the north side of the harbour, and in 1783 a tax of half a crown was levied on all these machines, which had multiplied exceedingly. They were set on the beach so that at least 50 yards separated the sexes, and the hiring fee of 18 pence included provision of umbrella, guidebook, and bathing dress. With the seven or eight visits of George III the town became almost as fashionable as Bath, and many of the handsome Georgian buildings along the Esplanade date from this period. The grateful townsfolk also erected a quite monstrous statue of King George, which disfigures the sea front to this day, but grateful they might well be, for the popularity of Weymouth for holidays has never declined. Its Georgian decor was modified later by the Victorians, but in the context accept-ably, for this is the Victorian England of the pierrot show, and Punch and Judy on the beach, and the concert party on the pier. In season, all this, though in modern dress, is still largely there. The sharpest reminder of it out of season is the little clock tower commemorating the Queen's golden jubilee, very gay and cheer-ful in its smart blue, red, and gilt paint.

The town's two main churches are both of the early nineteenth century. Holy Trinity, on the Weymouth, or southern, side of the harbour is an impressively spacious and well proportioned building of 1836, while St. Mary's, in St. Thomas Street in what was Melcombe Regis, was constructed in 1816 on the site of a seventeenth-century church that the parish had outgrown. It contains an altarpiece by Sir James Thornhill, who was born at Melcombe Regis in 1675. He was appointed history painter to George I in 1720. In 1730 his daughter, then aged 18, eloped with Hogarth, to whom he objected, at least as a son-in-law. In the following year his wife showed him some of the engravings their daughter's husband had produced for 'The Harlot's Progress', which he duly admired. When he learned the artist's name, he said, 'Very well; the man who can furnish representations like these can also maintain a wife without a portion.' Reporting this, Walpole says, 'He designed this remark as an excuse for keeping his purse-strings close; but soon after became both reconciled and generous to the young couple.'

Immediately to the north, Weymouth has absorbed several vil-lages with long histories. Radipole, at the head of the extensive backwater which bears its name, just where the river Wey flows into it, is still a small village, though with modern suburban style additions. Its curious little church, a diminutive bell tower at its west end, has an old timber roof, and fifteenth-century transepts. It stands on a knoll consorting closely with the seventeenth-century manor house.

At Upwey, similarly a mixture of old and new, just by the village school is a pellucid spring in a green dell, commercialised as 'The Only Genuine Wishing Well in Southern England'. The church is partly perpendicular, with some excellent gargoyles on the north side, and a Jacobean pulpit. East of the Dorchester road, and very remote, is the hamlet of Bincombe, walled in by the steep downs on three sides, and of interest chiefly for the simple church (parts of which were built in the thirteenth century), for the barrows on Bincombe Hill, and for the views from its summit.

Immediately south of Weymouth the Isle of Portland lies. Much more deserving than Purbeck to be called an island, it is none the less connected with the rest of Dorset by the Chesil Beach, which from this point of view becomes an extraordinarily elongated isthmus, separated from the mainland by the Fleet. The road from Weymouth crosses the narrow mouth of this strange inlet by a bridge, then becomes a causeway running by the side of the Chesil Bank and along a grey wall until it reaches the island at Chesilton, on the outskirts of Fortuneswell, the chief settlement. This little town clings to a hillside that rises from sea level to a height of 400 feet in just over a mile of twisting road, the grey houses in each street looking on to the roofs of their southern neighbours. At the very top is the Verne Fortress, built by convict labour in the nineteenth century, and now in use as a prison training centre (the former convict prison, at Grove, is today a Borstal). From the top of the hill the views are most exciting—eastward the coast as far as St. Aldhelm's Head, westward, the perfect yellow curve of the Chesil Bank curling round the bay like a scythe, on the horizon the hills of west Dorset, and to the north the rough hexagon of Portland Harbour, once one of the British Grand Fleet's more important anchorages, and still in use by the Royal Navy. At the foot of the hill on this northern side is Portland Castle, a blockhouse built by Henry VIII and complemented by Sandsfoot Castle, on the shore at Weymouth. Sandsfoot is a ruin now, the cliff on which it stands crumbling into the sea, but Portland Castle remains intact in the care of the Ministry of Works. To the south, lies a bare, despoiled country that sinks very gradually to the Bill, the island's southern tip. The villages of Easton, Weston, and Southwell, have broad streets with wide pavements, and houses of the grey local stone. Between them is a treeless, blasted landscape scarred with quarries, untidy, unkempt, and unprepossessing. The drystone walls and the refuse from the quarries emphasise the bleakness of it all.

Near Easton trees—probably the only trees in Portland—shade the Pennsylvania Castle, built in 1800 for John Penn, the grandson of William Penn, and governor of the island. It is now a hotel. Nearby is Portland's oldest building, the Rufus, or Bow-and-Arrow, Castle, a ruin perched on a crag for all the world as if it had grown there, overlooking the little bay called Church Ope Cove. The beach here is pebbly with light grey stones, and on either side are enormous, jagged boulders. People have set beach huts in this inhospitable spot, probably because it is less forbidding than the rest of Portland. A little seventeenth-century cottage at Easton, known as Avice's cottage because of Hardy's use of it in *The Well-beloved*, was given to the island as a museum by Marie Stopes the pioneer of birth control.

At the Bill man has done his worst to destroy the landscape. Near the old lighthouse, now a bird observatory, and once the home of Marie Stopes, a black rash of timber huts clusters. Further on are a huge car and coach park and scrappy buildings (restaurant, kiosk, toilets). Only the sea's very edge retains any of the grandeur this bare promontory must once have had. The lighthouse stands a few yards from the cliff, which here is only 20 feet above sea level, but below the cliff top are broad rock platforms formed by quarrying, their floors in places strewn with great boulders rounded by the sea to look like pebbles on a beach under an enormous magnifying glass. At the very tip of Portland is the curious Pulpit Rock, a knob of limestone against which rests a slab with footholes. To complete the desolation, just to the north is a bare brick building surrounded by barbed wire (a Ministry of Defence property) and beyond it a radio station with the inevitable masts. Four miles out to sea the Shambles, a sandbank marked by a light ship, has caused a host of wrecks, including that of the *Abergavenny* with the loss of 300 lives in 1805. Her commander, who went down with her, was the brother of the poet Wordsworth. Further to the west the current known as Portland Race sets in, and flows as far east as St. Aldhelm's Head.

Perhaps the one building on Portland of any architectural importance is the Church of St. George, Reforne, which stands in a bleak and exposed place near Easton, surrounded by a forest of elaborate and fantastic gravestones, largely overgrown and bramble-ridden. Once it was the parish church, but it is only used now as a cemetery chapel. A large building of grey ashlar, it has a west tower with a cupola, and a dome over the crossing, while its elegant and splendid interior includes box pews, twin pulpits, and galleries in both transepts as well as at its west end. It is quite the finest eighteenth-century church in Dorset.

If Purbeck was relatively isolated in the past, Portland was so almost absolutely, but despite its seclusion it has been inhabited for a long time. Roman remains—coins, coffins, and slingstones—have been found on it, and the Saxons settled it, only for the Danes to lay it waste in 787, 837, and 982. In Doomsday it was a Royal Manor, and has remained so, still holding its ancient Court Leet. Its people in their isolation for centuries kept their old idiosyncratic ways, such as their system of equal inheritance by all the sons of a man who died intestate, and the cheap, simple system of transferring ownership of land called 'church gift'. In medieval times they were famous for their prowess with the sling (whence Hardy called Portland the Isle of Slingers). Until the nineteenth century they even had their own marriage custom, 'that the man never marries' (as Hutchins puts it) 'till his intended wife is pregnant, and it was hardly ever broken in the memory of man but when the woman falsely assures the man that she was breeding'.

The fame of Portland stone as building material is usually dated from the time of Inigo Jones, who used it for the Banqueting Hall in Whitehall. Wren used it extensively in London after the Great Fire. A host of public buildings in the capital, from St. Paul's Cathedral and Waterloo Bridge downwards, are constructed of Portland stone, and so are many large buildings all over the country. Among the by-products of the quarries are impressive fossils, in particular ammonites sometimes as large as motor-coach wheels.

In the seventeenth century Portland gave London more than building stone. A concoction was made of the tubers of cuckoo-pint, which was thought on the evidence of its appearance alone, to be an aphrodisiac and tonic. Large quantities were sent from Portland to London, where it was regarded as a substitute for arrowroot, and was popularly known as Portland sago or Portland arrowroot. Portland's other major export was the flesh of its own breed of sheep, which Treves reported 60 years ago were still grazed on a common land in places. They have now disappeared completely.

Perhaps the final bizarre word on this bizarre island may rest with Hutchins. 'In November, 1457', he says, 'in Portland, was seen a cock coming out of the sea having a great crest on its head, a great red beard, and legs half a yard long. He stood on (*sic*) the water and crowed three times, and every time turned

himself about and beckoned with his head north, south, and west. He was in colour like a pheasant, and when he had crowed he vanished'.

The road from Weymouth westward to Abbotsbury, once clear of Chickerell, rolls through superb undulating country, with the coastal plain, the Fleet, and Chesil Bank freely visible, well below it to the south. Chesil Bank in fact runs for about 18 miles, from Chesilton to West Bay, but only from Abbotsbury eastward is it actually separated from the mainland. One can walk the entire distance, and I believe some masochists have done it. At the western end its stones are tiny, and one walks with great labour, as on soft sand. The size of the pebbles increases the further east one travels, until at Chesilton they are as big as goose eggs, and the sheer discomfort of walking on them for any distance is proportionate.

Rarely, the sea at its most aggressive has been known not to breach the bank, but to flow over it. It did so in November, 1824, when it swept a 90 ton sloop, the *Ebenezer*, on to the crest of the bank, and engulfed the little village of East Fleet. A group of cottages stands there now, next to the chancel, which is all the sea left of the old church. This little relic of grey rubble, half covered in ivy, still contains two brasses to members of the Mohun family, for this is the setting of John Meade Faulkner's adventure story, *Moonfleet*. The author is commemorated by a brass tablet on the south wall. The 'new' church, a quarter of a mile to the north-west, was built in 1829 in a setting which has grown almost unbelievably romantic, surrounded now by great trees in a dark grove, its grey ashlar smeared with a warm russet lichen. At this early stage of the Gothic revival architects retained something of the eighteenth-century feeling for proportion and both inside and out everything about this church is right.

Apart from the *Ebenezer* which in any case was re-launched in

15 *Bridport, looking west along the coast at West Bay*

the Fleet after some months, many ships were lost on the Chesil Beach in the days of sail. The local people, particularly the Portlanders, made strenuous efforts not so much to rescue the unfortunates aboard the wrecks, but to plunder them. The custom went back to medieval grants of the right to 'wreck of the sea' which were frequently made to landowners or even corporate bodies. So (to cite two instances of many), Henry II allowed Cerne Abbey to collect all wreckage on the shores of its lands bordering on the sea, and Henry III gave the same privilege at Kingston to the Abbess of Shaftesbury. 'Wrecking' then became a local occupation as easily tolerated by ordinary folk as smuggling, and its proceeds similarly shared in by all strata of the community.

Leaving aside Langton Herring and Rodden, which lie among the hills that fringe the Fleet, the only village between Chickerell and Abbotsbury is Portesham, where cottages of thatch and grey stone like large dolls' houses with miniature gardens line narrow lanes, and a stream of crystal clear water gushes past the fifteenth-century church. Nearby was the birthplace of Sir Thomas Hardy, Nelson's Flag Captain, to whom an excessively ugly monument, a grey tower like a factory chimney with a crinoline, was erected in 1844 on Blackdown Hill, to the north. The site, now owned by the National Trust, commands incomparable views in all directions, in a district which is thick with evidence of prehistoric occupation. The Hardy Monument, indeed, is a landmark visible from half of Dorset. A road clinging to the edge of the hills runs from Portesham to Upwey past Waddon Manor, an elegant remnant of a Queen Anne house, once occupied by Col. Bullen Reymes, a friend of Pepys. Further east, down a turning easily missed, is Corton Farm, the old farmhouse of grey stone (once three cottages, now unified) accompanied by a little Early English chapel which boasts a great rarity, a pre-Reformation stone altar.

All roads drops fairly steeply into Abbotsbury, which lies in the valley of the rivulet from Portesham and rather less than a mile from the sea shore, where Chesil Bank separates itself from the mainland. A large village with long if narrow and winding streets, its thatch and golden stone have seen much prosperity in its days of importance. Traditionally a church was built here in Roman or immediately post-Roman times, and in Saxon days it belonged to the abbey of Glastonbury. About 1044 one Orc, a house-carl of Canute's with his wife Thola, founded a Benedictine monastery, which flourished until the Dissolution. Some of its ruins are still visible south of the village. Parts of a gatehouse are incorporated in a cottage, stark walls tower over a green sward marked with traces of a building's outline. The great tithe barn (over 90 yards long), built about 1400, survives still partly intact. Half is roofless, the rest still in use, though the roof is now thatched, not stone-tiled as it used to be. On the threshing floor is an elderly threshing machine unemployed for many decades, but once worked by water power whose only surviving trace is the cavity outside in which the wheel turned.

The church, largely fifteenth and sixteenth centuries (and one of Dorset's most interesting), has some excellent features and fittings, including a west gallery, a Jacobean pulpit showing Civil War bullet holes, and a charming plastered barrel roof in the chancel (dating from 1638). The second window in the south aisle contains a fragment of late fifteenth- or early sixteenth-century glass representing St. Catherine or perhaps a Madonna, gently sorrowful, hands clasped, eyes downcast, an image of submissive grief. The manor house, opposite the church, is a pleasant and unpretentious Elizabethan building, with seventeenth-century additions, and some of the houses in the village incorporate stones obviously originating in the abbey.

At the top of a hill to the south is the small chapel of St. Catherine, built by the abbey in the late fourteenth century. The sea air and the rain have so pitted and fretted its golden local stone that it looks almost like a natural outcrop that the elements have carved into the form of a chapel, tall and stoutly buttressed.

The Ministry of Works are responsible for its upkeep, and at the moment of writing the interior is a confusion of rubble and scaffolding because of extensive restoration work, which may continue for some time. The elaborate roof vaulting, the main point of architectural interest in the chapel, is the particular object of attention, but the Ministry have also placed a wooden staircase in the beacon turret, whose original stone stairs had collapsed. The site is magnificent—below and to the south-east Chesil Bank and the Fleet, westward and northward the gentle green hills, and on the nearer slopes a profusion of lynchets. The swannery, open to the public at times, existed at least as early as 1373, and the sheltered tropical gardens are also to be visited in the summer.

The Abbey lands came after the Dissolution to Sir Giles Strangways, whose descendants still own them. The Strangways built a house from the stones of the abbey, but in 1644 Ashley-Cooper and his Roundheads descended on Abbotsbury and in the fierce and bitter skirmish which resulted not only were those bullets fired that scarred the pulpit in the church (which Col. James Strangways had garrisoned) but the house itself was destroyed when the Royalists' powder magazine blew up.

A mile and a half along the Bridport road Abbotsbury Castle, an unimpressive bivallate Iron Age hill fort accessible from a side road, offers splendid views along the coast, westward to Golden Cap, eastward along the sweep of Chesil Bank, with the enormous end-stop of Portland blocking the distance. North of the village, to be reached by footpath off the road to Hardy's Monument, lie two relics older still. One is the Grey Mare and her Colts, a most imperfect chambered long barrow on the crest of a hill. At the eastern end a few sarsen stones stand or lean crazily like stumps of petrified trees, and what is left of the earth mound stretches westward like an early morning shadow. The Grey Mare, the only certain example of this class of monument in Dorset, is all of 4,000 years old. The Kingston Russell stone circle, almost a mile further on, is less old, but not much less. Its stones, all fallen long ago, lie in a ring about 80 feet across in a cornfield and surrounded as they are by cultivated ground, but with meadow grass between them, they lend the site a magical quality as though they marked the boundary of a giant fairy ring.

CHAPTER FOUR

West Dorset

It is Bridport, if anywhere, that deserves to be regarded as the centre of western Dorset. Not only is it the most populous and thriving settlement near the coast west of Weymouth, but five of the major roads of the area converge upon it, and as the headquarters of the rope and netting industry, that has flourished in and around it since the Middle Ages, its demands for flax and hemp decisively influenced the economy of this part of the county until the nineteenth century.

It lies about a mile and a half from the mouth of the River Brit, which comes down from the hills north of Beaminster, and meets two tributaries, the Simene and the Asker, respectively in and south of Bridport itself. The old town fundamentally forms a T along three roads, South Street, coming up from the sea to meet West Street, which leads to Charmouth, and East Street, the road to Dorchester. At their junctions is the red brick town hall, built in 1785-6. The arcading originally accommodated a street market, and the little clock tower above, embellished with a cupola and weather vane, is a conspicuous landmark in a town of low buildings. In all directions from here except to the south green hills form a background to the townscape which they seem both to overshadow and protect.

Bridport wears eighteenth-century dress, but its history is longer than its appearance suggests, for it was already a sizeable town in the time of Edward the Confessor, when it had a mint, a priory and 120 houses. Its first charter it received from Henry III, but it was not actually incorporated until the reign of Henry

VIII, though this should not be assumed to indicate Royal indifference or disfavour. The rope industry first appears in a record of 1211, and a letter from King John to the sheriffs of Dorset and Somerset expressly instructs them to obtain their supplies of rope from Bridport. The Tudor antiquary, Leland, writes that Bridport was famous for daggers, but he was misled. A multitude of criminals having died in a noose of rope made hereabouts, this instrument of execution became known as a Bridport dagger, an expression which no one interpreted for poor Leland. The demands of Henry VIII's navy gave Bridport rope makers work and wealth, and from Chideock to Abbotsbury and Beaminster the country folk grew hemp in large quantities for the people of Bridport to turn into rope. It was not until the nineteenth century that the industry came to rely on imported raw materials, and hemp ceased to be grown in Dorset. It still grows wild in this part of the county, where the soil is highly suitable for it, and so does flax, which began to be cultivated when Bridport started making sail-cloth in the eighteenth century. Apart from the factories (neither obtrusive nor noisome) where rope and netting are still produced, the industry has left its mark on Bridport in the form of its remarkably wide streets, where the twine, yarn, and ropes were hung out to dry after being spun and twisted in the long gardens behind the houses. In the seventeenth century the Navy began to make its ropes at Portsmouth and Woolwich, so that Bridport found itself compelled to fall back on manufacturing less heavy materials than were needed for ships of the line. None the less in the following century Newfoundland, which enabled Poole to avoid decline, came also to Bridport's help, through the demand for ropes and nets for its fishing industry. When this trade too fell off, the town's prosperity was sustained by the production again of lighter products, which continues at the present day.

It is from that burst of prosperity in the late eighteenth and early nineteenth centuries that much of Bridport's (as of Poole's) character stems. Apart from the Town Hall, many buildings of the period remain in the three principal streets. The two most interesting are the charming Unitarian chapel of 1794 in East Street, and the Methodist chapel (1838) in South Street. A particular feature of the latter is its possession of a Jacobean pulpit —the very one used by that great-grandfather of the Wesleys who was vicar of Charmouth during the Civil War. North of the town stands Downe Hall, the grandest monument of the eighteenth century in Bridport, although it suffered some additions and alterations at the end of the nineteenth.

Of earlier periods less survives than one would like. The parish church, impressive though it is, was probably not improved by a depressing Victorian restoration, in which the chancel was rebuilt and two bays added to the early Perpendicular arcades of the nave and aisles. South of the church a stone building known as the Chantry, which dates from the fourteenth or fifteenth century, is used as a house, though perhaps built for some other purpose. On the other side of the road, and nearer to the Town Hall, are the Friends' Meeting House and Almshouses, a little group of buildings of the fifteenth to seventeenth centuries, with eighteenth-century alterations, all in whitewashed stone and black woodwork, and arranged round a courtyard which one enters through a narrow passage. The inn where Charles II had a hurried meal after leaving Charmouth in his flight from the disastrous field of Worcester stands opposite the Town Hall in East Street, but now transmogrified into a chemist's shop.

In June 1685, a detachment of foot and horse from Monmouth's army at Lyme Regis attacked the Dorset militia at Bridport. Advancing under cover of a thick mist they passed the bridge at Allington, in the west of the town, and took immediate possession, after firing only one volley. The militia were rallied with difficulty by their commanders and prevailed upon to stand fast at the eastern bridge, where, having received another volley from the rebels, they fired back and killed two. Monmouth's cavalry turned tail immediately and galloped back to Lyme with a tale of disaster, but the infantry, though disturbed by their defection, retreated only as far as the Allington bridge and set an ambush. As irresolute as their opponents, however, the King's men merely re-occupied the town centre and bawled abuse at the rebels, who bravely responded in kind for a while, until they decided to go, and retreated in good order, leaving Bridport in King James' possession.

The museum, just south of the Town Hall, a little Tudor house of golden stone with a two-storeyed porch, contains a well-arranged collection of artefacts and natural specimens with bearing on the town and its countryside.

The road to the port of Bridport, called West Bay (curiously, since the coast here is by nature harbourless, shelterless, and bayless) runs through the flood plain of the meandering River Brit and is now flanked by a good deal of bungaloid ribbon development. The village of Bothenhampton, on a cul-de-sac east of the main road, has some pleasant groups of early nineteenth-century buildings, and the tower and chancel only of its old church, with an eighteenth-century reredos and altar piece. Its modern church, built in 1889, is unconventional and effective, its arches, which are transverse, springing from the level of the window sills.

West Bay one must confess to be a curiosity, however seriously it takes itself. For centuries attempts were made to establish a port at the mouth of the Brit, only to be frustrated time and time again by the sea's annoying habit of silting it up. In 1619 the establishment was so pitiably decrepit that the bailiffs and burgesses launched an appeal, by licence of James I, for £3,000, soliciting 'the benevolence of well-disposed persons for the re-edifying of their decayed ancient harbour or haven'. They succeeded in collecting one hundred marks (about £67) which they disconsolately used for the maintenance of a schoolmaster. A century later, they, or their descendants, were still in difficulties and by Act of Parliament in 1722 were authorised to restore their troublesome port, which, the preamble says, had been ruined because of 'a great sickness' which carried off the wealthy inhabitants, and because not only was the harbour choked with sand, but the piers had collapsed. Despite the Act, nothing was done until 1741, but in the following 15 years repairs were effected, and in the face of the odds and the cost West Bay has continued to behave as a seaport ever since. The Brit is made to flow into a basin, which it scours through an arrangement of hatches, and into the sea between two piers, the channel which separates them accommodating only craft of moderate size. Despite frequent battering by storms, and the presence of a sand bar just outside the harbour mouth, West Bay is still used on a small scale commercially.

Not content, moreover, with its performance as a harbour, as mystifying as the Indian rope trick, it sets out determinedly to become another Blackpool, complete with kiosks of garish merchandise, and ice cream. A large caravan and camping site blazes with the violent colours of modern camping equipment. Modernistic (I use the word pejoratively) chalets are lined up for sale, and westward an esplanade creeps like a choking tendril along the foot of West Cliff. On the east side of the Brit, one does find something of the early nineteenth century, the Bridport Arms Hotel and a few other plain and honest buildings offering welcome relief to an untidy mess of riotous philistinism.

On either side a fairly steep hill leads to the top of a cliff, called prosaically the East Cliff and the West Cliff. Of the two the East Cliff is the lower, though from its foot it towers like an overhanging precipice, its face sheer and apparently much higher than its maximum 100 feet. A rich ochre in colour, it is formed of Bridport sand, capped with inferior oolite, and ribbed with bands of calcareous sandstone. It has a texture as rich as its colour and a regularity that suggests a building by Gropius. One can make a most uncomfortable and tiring walk along its foot, where a beach of small pebbles is littered close to the cliff with occasional blocks of stone. Alternatively, a path leads over the cliff and down again to the shore near Burton Bradstock, where the River Bride flows into the sea through the beginning of the Chesil Bank. Unfortunately, the main feature of the view here, apart from the cliffs and the bank of shingle, is again a caravan site, literally on the beach. One can understand the attraction for people who like beaches and caravans, but aesthetically the result is deplorable. On the far bank of the river, which is shallow enough for children to play in, is the easternmost cliff of west Dorset, Burton Cliff, geologically similar to East Cliff, except that the inferior oolite becomes much more prominent. Between here and Portland, the Chesil Bank forms the coast. A dull footpath leads to Abbotsbury behind it, and it soon becomes a prison wall, for it blocks one's view of the sea on the one hand leaving on the other a flat, marshy, almost pathless plain between itself and the inviting hills some way inland. Burton Bradstock itself lies on the Bridport-Abbotsbury road in its own valley, sheltered from the sea by its own cliff. Although ominous signs of contemporary development are appearing to the west and north stone and thatch still predominate in the village, which the main road fortunately passes and does not pierce. The golden stone church was internally ravished in 1897.

The road as far as Abbotsbury, incidentally, is no less impressive than beyond it towards Weymouth. Swyre, the only village between Burton Bradstock and Abbotsbury, has little to recommend it, but Puncknowle, half a mile further inland and pronounced 'Punnle', is a piece of rural Dorset at its most attractive. Modern bungalows and some nineteenth-century brick have not touched the village centre, where thatch and grey-gold stone, glowing and warm, predominate. The church and the seventeenth-century manor house lie side by side across the street from the villagers' homes and the inn. On higher ground than the rest of the village, the church, with its pyramidal tower roof, looks taller than it really is, despite the accompaniment of a full-grown chestnut tree. Within, it has a simple Norman tower arch and chancel arch of the same period, above which are the remnants of some possibly fifteenth-century painting. Its Norman font appears to rest on another, amusingly carved with a face. Among several monuments to members of the Napper or Napier family is one on the south wall, undated, and identifiable only by the initials (Sr R.N.), but probably to Sir Robert Napier, and dating from about 1700. This carelessness of such detail is of a piece with the formidable mood of the trilingual inscription: 'Man is the dream of a shadow' (in Greek). 'We make no grandiloquent speeches, but we live' (in Latin). And then in brusque English, 'Reader, when as thou hast done all thou canst thou art but an unprofitable servant. Therefore this marble affords no roome for fulsome flattery or vaine praise.' This same Sir Robert Napier set up in the church at Swyre a much more verbose monument to his relation, James Napier, who died in 1692, setting out at length the descent of the Napiers from 'the ancient family of Lenox of Scotland'.

Puncknowle is sheltered from the sea by a round hill, about 600 feet high, called the Knoll, with a choice view in all directions. To the north the valley of the Bride is crossed by the road to Chilcombe, a name which appears on no signpost that I have discovered. This lane, running from near Puncknowle to the Bridport-Dorchester road near Askerswell, is one of the few remaining public roads across which gates are closed to prevent cattle straying from unfenced fields, so that motorists must every now and again stop and open them if they wish to pass. Chilcombe is simply a farm and a twelfth- to fifteenth-century church, literally in the farmyard, of which its north wall forms one side. It is still in use as a church, and its interior shows every sign of care. On the north wall is an extraordinary poker-work panel traditionally a spoil of the Armada representing the Crucifixion in a style that looks oriental. The site is superb, overlooking the Bride valley, and sheltered from the north by Chilcombe Hill, on which lies an earthwork said to be a hill fort.

Still south of the main Dorchester road are three villages of more substance, Litton Cheney, Long Bredy, and Little Bredy. At the last of these the Bride rises, in the grounds of Bridehead, a crenellated Gothic house of the early nineteenth century in golden stone. The river is dammed to form a broadly serpentine lake to the south of it, and part of the parkland, planted with trees deciduous and evergreen, is open to the public on condition that they control their dogs, leave no litter, and make a donation to the church fabric fund. The church, rebuilt by Ferrey, looks its best from the valley below, where the river, tumbling to freedom over a waterfall, flows along the village street. To the north of the three villages and along the main road the hills (and north of the Bride we are back to chalk again) are prolifically studded with barrows and other earthworks, including on Martin's Down, north of Long Bredy, an excellent example of a form peculiar to south Dorset, a bank barrow.

Kingston Russell House, between Little Bredy and Long Bredy, as it stands today dates from the seventeenth and eighteenth centuries, and is conspicuous downhill from the public road as a Palladian building in Portland stone—at least, on its west side, for its older east front dates from the seventeenth century. The manor of Kingston Russell was given to a predecessor, possibly an ancestor, of the Russell family by William the Conqueror 'to be held by service of being marshal of the buttery', and in the reign of Edward I a William Russell held it not only as the King's cupbearer but also 'by service of counting the King's chessmen in his chamber, and returning them to their place when the King has finished his game'. The Russell male line here seems to have died out before the end of the fifteenth century, but another branch of the family continued to occupy the estate of Berwick, near Swyre, and it was from this branch that the Dukes of Bedford are descended. The story of the beginning of their fortunes appears in the next chapter. The second Earl of Bedford bought back the manor of Kingston Russell in the reign of Elizabeth, but it was one of the family of Michel, who carried out the radical re-building of the early eighteenth century. J. L. Motley, the American historian, died on a visit here in 1877.

To the west of Bridport and West Bay is a green land of strangely shaped hills, small villages, withdrawn valleys, and a majestic seaboard. From Bridport to Lyme Regis the Exeter road switchbacks over some of the steepest gradients on any of Dorset's main roads (west of Chideock, for instance, and again west of Charmouth) and takes in some excellent scenery, to be viewed at its best out of the holiday season. The range of hills, which borders the sea with variegated cliffs, is penetrated by streams in whose valleys lie the small towns and villages, supported today largely by the tourist trade—Eype, Chideock, Charmouth, and Lyme Regis. The first of these, Eype (pronounced Eep), in itself has little interest, but a narrow road winds to the sea at Eype Mouth, where one's car may be parked in a field perhaps 50 feet above sea level, and a tiny stream tumbles to the beach among slabs of rock to vanish into the shingle in a most uncanny fashion. The beach consists of small pebbles, and the cliffs are of grey clay. One may walk here from West Bay either over the cliff by a fairly easy path (though it is diverted by landslips at the western end), or along the beach, which is less comfortable at first because of loose shingle, but becomes easier the farther one travels from West Bay. The cliff-top walk is scenically the more attractive, the view westward dominated by Thorncombe Beacon and its sister cliffs, Doghouse Hill and Down (or Ridge) Cliff. They all jut aggressively into the Channel, but Thorncombe Beacon itself, tipped at its peak with yellow sandstone, rears up like a grey and gold fortress. Unfortunately, the caravan and camping site at Eype, commendably hidden though it is from the cliff, beach and road there, is horribly obtrusive from the east. The walk from Eype Mouth to the summit of Thorncombe Beacon is fairly easy but the ascent in the opposite direction, from the next gap in the cliffs, at Seatown, yields a sumptuous climax of cliff tops, first Ridge Cliff, then Doghouse Hill, then Thorncombe Beacon itself, in order of height, so that one rises by stages. The view eastward from the top is particularly fine. At Seatown itself, a dull collection of buildings redeemed by its setting, a little river called the Winniford, though larger than the brook at Eype Mouth, none the less disappears into the shingle in exactly the same way.

Half a mile north of Seatown is the village of Chideock (pronounced Chiddock) which the main road has spoiled, but not utterly ruined. It has cob and stone cottages, some thatched, some colour-washed, and a church heavily restored and much more attractive outside than in, with its embattled fabric of golden stone. It contains a black marble tomb of a knight, said to be Arundel. In the time of their greatness in the time of Elizabeth this family, which acquired the manor of Chideock by marriage in the fifteenth century, were staunch Catholics and shelterers of priests. Some way east of the church and north of the road is a field containing earthworks which are all that remain of their seat, Chideock Castle. Much of the moat is visible, though filled in on the north side and on a mound in the centre of the site stands a simple wooden cross bearing a plaque recording that the castle was built by Sir John de Chideock in 1380, and taken and destroyed by Parliament in 1645, and that from its gates five Catholic martyrs were taken to execution.

West of Seatown the cliffs reach their culmination. A footpath somewhat rudimentary in places leads up to the top of Golden Cap, the highest cliff along the whole of the south coast of England, reaching 617 feet at its summit. From below it looks romantically colourful, its grey face, called Wear Cliff, lumbering up in rugged steps from sea level, showing every evidence of landslips over its core of clay, to the thick coping of golden upper greensand, on which lie turf, gorse, and heather. On a sunny day in high summer the product is a brilliant contrast with the generally sombre seaboard. From the plateau at the top the view stretches from Portland (past the triple cliffs beyond Seatown, like three-teeth of a titanic shark) westward to Beer Cliff and Torbay. Inland, range upon range of hills fade into remote corners of three counties.

Below the western slope of Golden Cap lies the stricken little ruined chapel of St. Gabriel, roofless, overgrown, and bereft of its village. Built in the thirteenth century as a chapel of ease to Whitchurch Canonicorum it has been disused since 1841, when a new chapel was built at Morcombelake, but survives as a solitary relic. Incidentally, it is accessible by car only along a very rough track, but the country is excellent for walking, and appropriately enough is in the protection of the National Trust, which has covenanted rights along the six miles of coast between Eype and Charmouth. The cliffs from Seatown to Charmouth are liable especially after heavy rain to fairly frequent falls, and small streams plunge down the cliff face to dribble seaward through the shingle at the bottom and expose large quantities of fossils. The green ammonite beds which form the base of Golden Cap are rich especially in *Androgynoceras lataecosta*, the chamber of whose shells are found filled with green calcite, whence the name given to the parent rock.

Nearer Charmouth, below Stonebarrow, where the cliff engagingly called Cain's Folly is crowned also with upper greensand, the lower rocks are very rich in belemnites, and pyritised ammonites like dusky gold commonly reward the careful searcher on the beach.

Charmouth, like Chideock and Bridport, bestrides the main road a little way from the coast, though nearer to it than either of the other two. It lies, like all the coast towns of west Dorset, in a gap in the coastal hills, this time on the right bank of the river Char. It has grown up the fairly steep side of the valley, so that the road to Lyme and Axminster clambers sharply out of it, with unpleasing consequences in the holiday traffic of the summer.

It was the scene of heavy fighting with the Danes in the ninth century, yet, historically, Charmouth's moment of glory

came after the Battle of Worcester, when Charles II, routed by Cromwell, fled into Dorset in the hope of escaping to France. He had taken refuge with a Royalist gentleman, Col. Wyndham, of Trent. A certain Stephen Limbry, of Charmouth, was persuaded to undertake the transport of an anonymous Royalist officer over the Channel for £60. Accordingly, rooms having been found at the Queen's Arms in Charmouth, Charles came from Trent disguised as a groom, accompanied by Miss Juliana Coningsby riding pillion, Lord Wilmot as her lover, and Col. Wyndham and his servant Peters as guides. Wilmot and Miss Coningsby sat affectionately in the parlour while Charles busied himself with the horses. Wyndham and Peters went down to the sea to await Limbry. Unfortunately for the conspirators Limbry had married a woman of strong character who, having read the proclamation threatening death to anyone who assisted Charles, and suspecting the identity of the officer her husband had undertaken to convey, locked her spouse in his room and hid his trousers. So Wyndham and Peters had to go back frustrated to their party and make fresh plans.

Charles, Miss Coningsby, and Wyndham, it was decided, should return to Trent via Bridport, where they were to meet Wyndham and Peters, who stayed behind to find out why Limbry had failed them. Meanwhile, the ostler at the Queen's Arms, a Roundhead soldier with his wits about him, began to entertain suspicions of Charles' party and went to discuss them with the parson, Bartholomew Wesley, whose pulpit is now in Bridport. That worthy, being at family prayers, refused to see the caller who for reasons best known to himself failed either to press his case with Wesley or to inform the Cromwellian officer in the town. Charles therefore got away, Wesley ruefully observing afterwards that if the king were restored, 'he would love long prayers, for had he (Wesley) not been longer than ordinary at his devotion he had surely snapt him'.

Now Wilmot's horse having cast a shoe, was taken to the

blacksmith, who observed that each of the three remaining shoes had been set in a different county, including one in Worcestershire. This was enough for the ostler. He went back to the parson, Clucking and bustling officiously Wesley astonished the landlady at the Queen's Arms by calling her a Maid of Honour, since Charles Stuart 'lay last night at your house and kissed you at his departure, so that now you cannot but be a maid of honour'. 'If I believed', the woman replied, 'it was the King, as you say it was, I would think the better of my lips all the days of my life'. Wesley then approached a local Justice, who refused to believe Charles was in the district and took no action. Even now the ostler failed to report to the military authorities for several hours, and when he did so, and the hunt began, the royal party had several hours start, and Charles was successfully brought away.

The Queen's Arms has not remained an inn uninterruptedly since that time, and in the early years of this century at least it was divided into two houses. Now, however, it is again a hotel, though not a tavern, a building of the early sixteenth century, for which is claimed not only Charles' adventure, but a visit by Catharine of Aragon.

The Char, which rises south of Broadwindsor and drains the Vale of Marshwood, meanders through meadows to the sea between Stonebarrow and Black Ven, half a mile south of Charmouth. A field on the right bank is used as a car park, the road to which from the village is narrow, but green with gardens. Black Ven, the furthest west of the great hills of the Dorset coast, raises its multicoloured terraces—green, gold, grey, and blue—sharply from sea level to form a barrier between Charmouth and Lyme Regis. The argillaceous grey rock to which it gives its name, Black Ven marls, contains deposits of iron pyrites, and in 1908 a fall and the consequent sudden exposure of a mass of this material caused enough oxidation to make the bituminous shale burn, with the production of clouds of smoke.

The phenomenon was sensationally called the Lyme volcano. The blue lias rock underlying the marls comes to the surface nearer Lyme itself, and contains abundant fossils of ammonites, fish, and ichthyosaurus. Of these last the first complete specimen ever discovered was unearthed in 1811 by Mary Anning, a schoolgirl only 12 years old. Born in 1799, she was the daughter of a carpenter, who made a little extra money by selling fossils as curios to visitors. Mary and her brother Joseph helped him, and continued the work after their father's death in 1810. In fact, it seems that it was Joseph who found the head of the ichthyosaurus, and Mary who uncovered the rest of the skeleton. But most of the work was Mary's, she became a celebrity overnight, and the specimen was sold to the Lord of the Manor for £23. For her this was not the end. She found in 1824 an almost perfect plesiosaurus, and four years later the first pterodactyl skeleton ever found in Britain. Scholars visited Lyme merely to converse with her, and the King of Saxony called at her shop, to be told calmly (and truthfully): 'I am well known throughout the whole of Europe'. Indeed her death from cancer in 1847 was described by a local writer as 'in a pecuniary sense, a great loss to the town', since she brought it so many eminent visitors. The Royal Geological Society and local subscribers set up a window to her (a little shabby today) in the parish church of her birthplace.

Lyme is squeezed into a narrow gap at the mouth of the little River Lym which looks altogether too small, vivaciously as it gushes down its miniature canyon through the town centre, ever to have cut a valley big enough to contain a town. Perhaps contain may be the wrong word, for Lyme spreads up the sides of its surrounding hills, precipitous though they and the roads down them are. The place has been settled at least since 774, when Cynewulf, King of the West Saxons, granted land here for the extraction of salt by boiling sea water. The manor in the Doomsday survey is recorded as divided among the Bishop of Salisbury, Glastonbury Abbey, and one William Belet, but later it reverted wholly to the crown, and Edward I gave it a charter in 1279. He is the *rex* of the town's name. At first it prospered, sending four ships to the siege of Calais in 1347, but in the fifteenth century it suffered severely from the depredations of the French, like Melcombe and Poole.

It was in the reign of Edward I that the famous Cobb was originally built, probably of wood. It serves as a quay and a groin, the coast hereabouts being by nature as innocent of shelter as further east at West Bay, and without it Lyme's history as a port could never have been written. On numerous occasions the sea has breached it or broken it down entirely, the most notorious if not the most disastrous pounding occurring in the great storm of November, 1824. In the course of the centuries its shape has altered several times, and for some periods it was no more than a breakwater. An observer in the reign of Charles II remarked that its stones were not cemented, so that the waves flowed 'in and out through the interstices of the stone in the most wonderful manner'.

Lyme reached its zenith as a commercial port in the late sixteenth and early seventeenth century, when it traded extensively with Guinea, Spain, Portugal, and the East and West Indies. A native of Lyme, Sir George Somers (who is buried in Whitchurch Canonicorum) was wrecked in 1609 on a reef off Bermuda, which he was wrongly credited with discovering, and which was at the time called after him. At the outbreak of the Civil War Lyme declared for Parliament like the other Dorset ports, and in 1644 endured a two months' siege by a Royalist army under the command of Prince Maurice, who failed to take the town despite his superiority in numbers and advantages in position. Among those commanding the defence was Lt. Col. Blake, better known for his victories at sea during the Protectorate, but doubtless responsible at least in part for the vigour with which the defence was conducted. The Roundheads beat off assault after assault, occasionally reinforced and supplied by sea, until the approach of the Earl of Essex with an army from Dorchester caused

Maurice to withdraw, baffled. Parliament recognised the effort that had been made, voting £2,000 to the town, with a supply of boots and shoes, and £150 to the governor.

The Duke of Monmouth's landing on the Cobb in 1685 pushed Lyme briefly into the floodlit centre of national affairs. Arriving with three ships after 19 days at sea delayed by unfavourable winds, the Duke set up his standard and a proclamation was read not only asserting his right to the succession, but also accusing King James of having poisoned Charles II. Recruits poured in, among them the young Daniel Defoe, more indeed than Monmouth could arm, and after the failure of his attempt on Bridport he marched out 3,000 strong to Axminster and ultimate catastrophe.

The War of the Spanish Succession marked the disruption of Lyme's trade, and the beginning of a decline reversed like that of Weymouth by the development of the sea-bathing cult. By the end of the eighteenth century it had established itself as a popular watering place and was a favourite of Jane Austen's, as readers of *Persuasion* know. The very steps down which Louisa Musgrove took her fateful tumble still lead from the lower to the upper Cobb, and buildings which still look to us much as they must have done to her and her creator remain in Church Street, Coombe Street, and Broad Street. Something of a slightly later period, say as late as 1850, also remains in this central part of the town, which is cheerful and snug with neat unpretentious pre-Victorian and early Victorian frontages, brightly colour-washed. A little group on the Marine Parade, weather-boarded, thatched, and bow-windowed is particularly noticeable.

The holiday industry has flourished for two centuries in Lyme, and she is no longer a commercial port. True, the Cobb wears a board with an impressively varied list of rates on merchandise charged in the port in 1879, including 40 items ranging from timber and coal to wine, horses, and butter, but the last major work on the harbour finished in 1853, and no ships of any size could now shelter there. Yachts are its modern caravels.

The parish church, on the edge of a cliff facing east, and above the bridge, where the Lym runs into the sea, and the town museum hoards its Monmouth relics and ammonites and bits of ichthyosaurus, has a forbidding appearance from the repellent brown stucco on the porch and tower. The interior is one of the most attractive in Dorset. The tower is Norman, and the porch was originally the nave. The transepts were probably destroyed when the church was enlarged to the east of the tower about 1500, by the building of the spacious Perpendicular structure that bears witness to Lyme's wealth and importance at the time.

For a town of its size, the list of eminent people born there is long. Apart from Sir George Somers it gave birth in the sixteenth century to Arthur Gregory, who became a trusted instrument of Sir Francis Walsingham, the brilliant organiser of Queen Elizabeth's intelligence service, and M.P. for Lyme. Gregory had a simple skill, in which he was perfect: 'he had the admirable art of forcing the seal of a letter', in the words of Thomas Fuller, 'so invisibly that it still appeared a virgin to the exactest beholder'. All packages to foreign ambassadors at Court were for years opened by Gregory to be read by Walsingham, then resealed and delivered. Capt. Thomas Coram, the creator of the Foundling Hospital from the fortune he made trading in pitch and tar to Virginia, was born in Lyme in 1668. Dr. John Case, a quack physician who in the latter half of the seventeenth century is said to have made more money from his remedies than Dryden did from his poems was also a native of Lyme Regis. He put on his door a sign which read,

> *Within this place*
> *Lives Doctor Case.*

Having made enough money to retire and live respectably, he adopted a coat of arms with the motto, 'The Case is Altered'.

Mary Anning has already been mentioned, but as a shrewd business woman she was matched by Mrs. Eleanor Coade, who may have been a native of Lyme herself and married a member of a well-known local family (a John Coade was mayor in 1779, and Cobb Road was once Coade's Road). In the later eighteenth century she perhaps invented, but certainly marketed an artificial stone, made of china clay, felspar, potash, and titanium oxide, fired at 1000°C, which was extensively used in public and private buildings all over the country. St. George's Chapel, Windsor, Stourhead, Somerset House, and the Brighton Pavilion, are just a few. The statue of George III at Weymouth is of Coade stone. In 1769 she and her husband moved to London and set up a factory at Pedlar's Acre, Lambeth, on the site of the Royal Festival Hall, where it survived (as a terracotta works) until 1949. Since business women were rare in her day, we can judge her to have been a person of unusual abilities, for it was she who supplied the acumen and energy which ensured the success of the stone. 'Belmont' on the corner of Cobb Street and Pound Road, stands on a site given to her by her husband's uncle in 1784, and part of this house, heavily ornamented on the north side with specimens of the product which made her fortune, was probably built for her. She died in 1796, aged 88.

The hinterland of Lyme and Charmouth is hilly, wooded, and thinly populated, and such villages as occur though pleasantly situated (even romantically, like Monkton Wyld, its Victorian church with spire and vulgarly ornate interior, set on a wooded hillside of nordic gloom) none the less without buildings or associations of outstanding interest. North of Wootton Fitzpaine the road cuts clean through the most westerly Iron Age fort in Dorset, Coney's Castle, half a mile from the Devon border over which is Lambert's Castle Hill, where another hill fort can be traced among the gorse clumps which largely cover its sour soil. A little further on is the hamlet of Marshwood, remarkable only for its situation on the very rim of the Vale to which it gives its name.

On the Vale's southern edge, north of the road from Charmouth to Chideock, Whitchurch Canonicorum ought not to be missed. The village is so scattered among the winding roads and wooded hills that the church seems almost detached from the substance of its parish. It stands on a knoll behind a group of brick cottages and a modern stone cross, its slender grey tower visible for some distance before one reaches it. Inside it really is a white church, not painted, but of white stone, the north arcade partly Norman, the south Early English and exquisite, with finely carved capitals. The Jacobean pulpit, the splendid tomb of Sir John Jeffrey, who died in 1611, the fifteenth-century roof of the nave, the whole building is full of such details to take the eye. Most remarkable of all, Whitchurch is the only parish church in England to possess the bones of its patron saint. She was a lady called Wite, Wita, or Candida, and her shrine, a simple stone chest with a Purbeck marble slab, and three pointed oval openings in the front, stands in the north transept. Owing to a settlement in the foundations at the turn of the century the interior was uncovered and found to contain a leaden casket housing the bones of a woman of about 40, its lid inscribed HIC REQI-ESCT RELIQIE SCE WITE. (Here rest the remains of St. Wite.) Nothing is known of her for certain. An over ingenious theory connects her with a Breton St. Blanche, but according to a local tradition she was a Saxon lady killed in a Danish raid. Whatever the truth, the church was a place of pilgrimage in the Middle Ages, when believers would place in the orifices in the shrine articles belonging to the sick to endow them with healing properties, or diseased limbs to cure them. The modern tourist cannot resist throwing coins, presumably for luck.

North of the main road and not far from Bridport lie several villages worth visiting. Symondsbury, a cluster of golden stone and thatch, has a church whose fourteenth-century crossing conveys an impression of determined weight and power. Outside, a superb lime tree dominates the road junction by the churchyard, and Colmer's Hill, quite conical, overlooks the whole scene.

Bradpole is now virtually a suburb of Bridport, but its church commands a pleasant view of green rolling hills. Less than a mile further on the village of Loders lies in a narrow valley by a stream, wedged between Boarsbarrow Hill and Waddon Hill, its crenellated and gargoyled church, spacious within and tactfully restored, showing something of all periods of architecture from the twelfth to the fifteenth century. The village houses, like those in other villages in this part of Dorset, are all of the same golden stone often with thatched roofs, the materials harmonising unobtrusively. The hills hereabouts are of oolite and the stone is local.

Beyond Askerswell the land rises sharply to Askerswell Down on the south and Eggardon Hill on the north. This steep and uncompromising mass, the western end of a long ridge of chalk, bears 800 feet above sea level a huge hill fort, 36 acres in extent, including the ramparts. To the north-east and south-west the hill drops away precipitously, and a landslip on the south-western side was followed by a strengthening of the defences there. Two elaborately defended entrances lie along the ridge, one at each end of the camp. The view from the ramparts into and across the valleys to north, south, and west is exhilarating.

The road beyond Eggardon runs north to the valley of the River Hooke, but a track leads westward to Powerstock and West Milton, and a stretch of country the equal of any in Dorset except the coast. To reach it by car from Bridport one must bear left in Bradpole or Loders, but it does not matter how you approach it: the important thing is to be there, in that superb, rolling countryside of steep-sided valleys twisting among fantastically shaped, lush green hills. West Milton lies in one of those green clefts, a stream running along the bottom south of the road. Its houses are again thatch on the yellow local stone. Its nineteenth-century church looks across the valley from the south slope of a hill, and much higher up at the other end of the village is just the tower of the old church (long replaced) set among a handful of table tombs in its churchyard. It commands a splendid view eastward to Eggardon. Further up the valley, Powerstock is a larger settlement at the confluence of two streams, and grown a little shapeless by the nature of its site. The church, which stands at a high central point, has a fifteenth-century doorway with weathered but still delicate niches and carvings, and a most ornate but asymmetrical Norman chancel arch. Above the village on a hill commanding the valleys of both streams and their junction is a motte-and-bailey earthwork which probably dates from the late eleventh or twelfth century. In the eighteenth some walls were still standing, but they had disappeared by 1865. Tradition said this was a winter palace of King Athelstan. We know King John had a house at Powerstock, and this may be its site. He visited it much less than Bere Regis, but in his time the country round about was a Forest in the care of the de la Lynde family, who also had charge of the royal hunting lands in Blackmore Vale.

The main road from Bridport to Beaminster, along the broader valley of the Brit, on its eastern side passes Ferrey's very authentic-looking and impressive Victorian Norman church at Melplash. Further north, on the same side of the road, is Melplash Court, a largely seventeenth-century house whose gardens are sometimes open to the public, approached down a straight avenue of chestnuts. It is a plain building of honey-coloured stone, and a large round stone dovecote in the same material stands near one corner, like a tower of a castle, much weathered and mottled with lichen.

The village of Netherbury lies off the Beaminster road among hills, and astride the Brit, a settlement of yellow stone houses with a pleasant church of the fourteenth and fifteenth centuries. Up river, and approached from the main road is the manor house of Parnham, for 300 years a seat of the Strode family, and now owned by the National Association for Mental Health. It is open to the public on Thursday afternoons in the summer. Largely built in the mid-sixteenth century it was altered in the eighteenth, and in 1810 received an addition designed by Nash. Since 1896, when it was sold for the first time, successive owners have altered the interior considerably, so that it has many features and fittings, brought often enough from elsewhere.

On Beaminster (pronounced Bemmister) all the books quote William Barnes' joyous lines,

> *Sweet Be'mi'ster, that bist a-bound*
> *By green and woody hills all round,*
> *Wi' hedges, reachen up between*
> *A thousan' vields o' zummer green . . .*

which, fortunately, still have some bearing on the town and its surroundings. West Dorset has changed much less than most of southern England in the last 150 years. Beaminster's encircling hills, for it is set in a bowl of oolitic uplands, are still green and woody, and give birth to the River Brit which has cut itself an exit southwards through them, past Parnham, on its way to Bridport. Consequently, however one approaches Beaminster, except from the south, one sees it first from above, and very pleasant it is to look upon. It is a place of mellow stone, honey-coloured and substantial-seeming, many of its buildings dating from the eighteenth or late seventeenth centuries, with just a few older by a hundred years or so. That no more survive is due to the usual cause, fire, which devastated Beaminster (like so many other Dorset towns) three times in two centuries. In 1644, a particularly destructive blaze occurred, when the Royalist army of Prince Maurice lay in the town. According to a contemporary account it began with the discharge of a musket in the gable of a house in North Street, 'and it was wild fire, and the wind directly with the towne, so the whole towne was destroyed in two hours. . . . There were seven score and four dwelling houses, besides barns and stables burnt.' Looting by the soldiery added to the burden of the citizens. Other conflagrations are recorded for 1684 and

1781, but on both of these occasions the damage appears to have been less serious.

The church survived, thanks to the exertions of the people, only to fall victim to the Victorian passion for renovation. That the restorers' energies were expended on the interior may be counted perhaps as fortunate, but as a result the fabric from outside promises so much more than it provides. The tower, the best in Dorset, remains, with its crenellations and pinnacles, its sculptured figures, its angel and beast corbels, in short with its look of having strayed out of Somerset. Inside, though, atmosphere has gone, with the old roofs, the old pews and gallery, and all those other details that in such churches as St. George's, Reforne, or Puddletown so powerfully evoke the past. Without them Beaminster church is impressive. With them it would have been priceless. It still has some good monuments (particularly that to Thomas Strode, who looks a very credible person apart from his fancy dress), a Jacobean pulpit, and a twelfth-century font.

Two miles away, to the south-east, at the head of a winding valley which leads a little stream to join the Brit near West Milton, is the Manor house of Mapperton, whose grounds are sometimes open to the public. Approached from the north, down an avenue of elms, the house is built in golden stone, mottled with grey and yellow lichen. The chimneys look like spirals of butterscotch, and so do the north wing finials on which sit heraldic beasts. The gardens are carefully designed to take advantage of the configuration of the land and the presence of the little river, which has been tamed into ponds and swimming pool in a carefully calculated setting. The church, which is attached to the house to form the third side of the entrance court, was built in 1704. In the reign of Edward I the manor was owned by the Brett family, from whom it passed by descent in the female line to the Morgans. One of these last, Robert Morgan, had special permission to wear his bonnet in the presence of Henry VI, 'forasmuch as we be credibly informed that . . . for various infirmities which he hath in his head, (he) cannot conveniently without his great danger be discovered of the same'. About a hundred years later another Robert Morgan rebuilt the house, though only the north wing. Its north front (classified in the eighteenth century) remains of his work. Richard Brodrepp owned the property after 1618 and rebuilt the main range, while the stables and coach houses date from about 1670.

Not far to the north-east is the source of the River Hooke, which flows eastward through the hamlets of Hooke, Toller Porcorum, and Toller Fratrum, to join the Frome near Maiden Newton. Toller Porcorum is named, according to Hutchins, from the large numbers of swine formerly maintained in the district, and has rejoiced in the alternative names of Swyne Toller and Hog Toller, as well as Great Toller. The church, which overlooks the village from a low hill, has a curious font, which may have been made from a Roman capital. Toller Fratrum lies at the end of a cul-de-sac off the Dorchester-Crewkerne road, and consists of little but the church and the manor, now a farm house. About 1300 it was owned by the Knights Hospitallers (whence its name, Toller 'of the Brothers') and after the Dissolution came to the Samways family of Winterborne St. Martin (or Martinstown). The manor was built about 1540 by John Samways, of grey and gold stone, with twisted chimneys and beast finials, including one carved as a chained monkey holding a mirror. This was the emblem of the Martyns of Athelhampton, near Puddletown, and may be a punning reference to them and to Samways' native village. The church was rebuilt in the nineteenth century, but has two relics of the twelfth. One is a small stone set in the east wall of the chancel, a sculptured relief representing the Magdalen wiping the feet of Christ with her hair. The other is the font, carved with an astonishing fantasia of heads and arms.

West of Beaminster, along a winding lane sunk deep between steep banks and high hedges is Stoke Abbot, a village of golden stone, a material as typical of west Dorset as light grey stone of the south-east or grey stone with flint bands of the centre. The simple church which overlooks a deep valley, green and wooded, with plain green hills opposite, was largely unspoiled by the Victorians and boasts a highly decorative twelfth-century font. From 1782-86 William Crowe was Rector here and there is a memorial tablet to him in the church porch. Crowe's fame rests (or rested) on his poem 'Lewesdon Hill' which he published in 1786.

This feature, almost 900 feet high, lies west of Stoke Abbot, and is twinned with Pilsdon Pen, the highest hill in the county, just a few feet more than 900 and a mile and a half further to the west. From the coast these two look so much alike that seamen used to call them 'the Cow and the Calf', and Dorset men would speak of things 'as much akin as Lewesdon Hill to Pilsdon Pen'. In fact they do differ. Lewesdon is round and wooded, Pilsdon *Which like a rampire bounds the vale beneath* elongated and bare but sloping gently westward towards Thorncombe. At the south-eastern end of Pilsdon, overlooking Marshwood Vale, is a multivallate hill fort whose ramparts are shaggy with spiny gorse. It was occupied at the time of the Roman conquest, and stormed by the invaders.

Within the Vale itself (which we have now circled completely) the settlements are tiny and scattered. The roads twist mysteriously through lush, clayey fields and tall hedges, sometimes without benefit of signpost. In Hutchins' day, and later, it was 'hardly passable by travellers but in dry summers', while Crowe describes it as

> Cold, vapourish, miry, wet, and to the flocks
> Unfriendly, when autumnal rains begin
> To drench the spungy turf. . . .

This is rich dairy country, home of the delectable blue vinney cheese, but most sparsely populated.

Pilsdon itself has its Elizabethan manor, a farm, and a Victorian church. Higher on the slope of Pilsdon Pen the small eighteenth-century manor house of Bettiscombe has survived two centuries in satisfyingly complete condition, with many of its original fittings still *in situ*. It is owned by descendants of John Pinney, who was Vicar of Broadwindsor during the Protectorate, and probably built this house about 1694. He died in 1705. The house can show an alleged secret passage, said to lead under Pilsdon Pen but probably an eighteenth-century drain, and a skull to which miraculous properties are attributed. It was supposed to be that of a negro slave, who, having been brought from the West Indies by a Pinney who made a fortune there, laid a curse on his master should he not be buried in his own country. Of course, when the slave died he was buried in the local churchyard, from which spectral screams accompanied a crop failure and other agricultural disasters. The body was therefore disinterred, but we are not told what happened to the rest of it. The legend says that no ghost will walk at Bettiscombe while the skull is there. Unfortunately for the gothic imagination, the skull is at least 1500 years old and probably Romano-British.

John Pinney left Bettiscombe to his son, Nathaniel, whose brother was transported to the West Indies for participation in the Monmouth Rebellion. It was this brother's grandson, John Frederick, who came back rich to Bettiscombe, which was held by his relative, Azariah, became M.P. for Bridport, and built a house of his own a mile or so away at Racedown, at the western end of Pilsdon Pen. Both he and Azariah dying childless, the property came to John Frederick's second cousin, John Pretor, who took the name Pinney. He added a third storey to Racedown, but himself lived in Bristol. From 1795-7 Racedown was lent to William and Dorothy Wordsworth, who thoroughly enjoyed their stay, according to Dorothy's letters. It was at Racedown that William wrote *The Borderers*. It is a very decent brick building with ashlar dressing, easily visible from the road just north of Birdsmoorgate.

At Broadwindsor the church is a pleasant-looking building in golden ashlar. Thomas Fuller was Vicar here fom 1635, but took the king's side in the Civil War, and John Pinney, a Parliamentarian, 'intruded', in the contemporary jargon, until the Restoration. But when, in 1660, Fuller came back with the flood tide of royalism, he was so pleased with Pinney's preaching that he told the parishioners that 'he would not deprive them of such a man'. The story is in character of one who would write: 'The last and only way to purge errors out, is in a faire and peacable way; for the sword cannot discerne betwixt truth and error; it may have two edges but never hath an eye'. Among Fuller's works were *The Holy War*, an important history of the Crusades, and his *Worthies of England*, which he wrote at Broadwindsor and which remains a useful source of biographical detail. As a keen bibliophile he took great interest in the physical appearance of his own works on publication. The pulpit he and Pinney used remains, still fulfilling its purpose, in the church, which is not the one he knew, having been rebuilt almost from its foundations in 1868.

The civil parish of Thorncombe forms a Dorset salient bounded by the Axe and Blackwater, jutting between Somerset and Devon, of which it was part until the mid-nineteenth century. Its countryside is gentler than most of the rest of west Dorset, though its lanes are deep-set and shaded, Devonshire fashion. Thorncombe village has a drab look. Its church, large for its village, entirely rebuilt in 1867, and otherwise dull, has a mainly sixteenth-century pulpit, and by far the best brass in Dorset— life-size effigies of Sir Thomas Brook and his wife Joan, who died respectively in 1419/20 and 1437. Sadborow, a mile or so to the south, where the gardens are occasionally open, is a fine house built in 1773-5 of Portland stone faced with Ham Hill stone ashlar. Inside, its entrance hall leads to a curving stone staircase under a most elegant dome.

On the northern edge of the salient, the River Axe flows past the grounds of Forde Abbey, in many ways the most attractive of all Dorset country houses, and fortunately open fairly often to the public during the summer. The spacious gardens contain a wealth of tall and splendid trees and flowering shrubs and lakes, and the house itself has a magnificence paralleled only in other counties. Its history begins in 1136, when Richard de Redvers, Earl of Exeter, founded a Cistercian abbey at Brightley near Okehampton for 12 monks from Waverly in Surrey. He died in the following year, and four years later, discouraged by the difficulties they encountered at Okehampton, the community decided to return to Waverly. On the way they passed through Thorncombe, inherited from Richard by his sister, Adelicia, who, moved by their plight, their connection with her brother, and doubtless by piety, handed over to them her house at Forde, 'where you now are, which is very fruitful and well-wooded, which I give you for ever in exchange for your barren land at Brightley. . . . Stay there until a more convenient monastery may be built for you upon some other part of the estate.' There indeed they stayed, until the abbey buildings were raised for them six years later. Adelicia died a short while after they arrived, but she bequeathed her interest in them to her descendants, the Courtneys of Shroton, who were patrons of the abbey for many years.

The earliest part of the surviving buildings is the chapel which, though now dominated by its seventeenth-century screen, originally was the chapter house, built in the time of the third Abbot, Baldwin of Exeter. As Archbishop of Canterbury after 1185 he crowned Richard I, accompanied him on his Crusade, and died of disease at Ptolemais in 1191. Abbot John of Devon, who held his office at Forde for 30 years, was chaplain and confessor to King John, and a scholar, of whom Fuller wrote, '. . . in his time Forde Abbey had more learning therein than three convents of the same bigness.' The long dorter range must have been built during or not long after his day.

The last Abbot, Thomas Chard, began to preside in 1521, and it is to him that we owe a great deal of the present building. The handsome entrance tower, the great hall (which retains its original panelled ceiling) and what is left of the cloisters are all his work. In 1539, Chard surrendered the Abbey to the Crown, his work unfinished, leaving the fan vaulting of his cloisters for an Elizabethan to finish off, with plaster not stone, and details elsewhere uncarved. One can only guess his feelings. The estate came then to Richard Pollard, son of Chief Justice Pollard, and was sold later to Sir Amyas Paulet, and then to the Solicitor-General, William Rosewell. In 1649 the legal connection continued with the purchase of Forde by Cromwell's Attorney-General, Sir Edmund Prideaux.

After the Dissolution the abbey church was demolished (a lawn south of the house covers its site) and with it the southern part of the cloister garth. But Prideaux had some alterations made, largely internally, and seems to have commissioned much of the woodwork and the plaster ceilings which give such distinction to the house today. The design of this work used to be attributed to Inigo Jones, almost certainly wrongly. The wonderfully carved staircase, the ceiling of the saloon on the first floor, and the chapel screen are three among many features dating from Prideaux', or his son's operations.

The son was unlucky enough in 1680 to entertain the Duke of Monmouth at Forde during his perfectly legitimate western progress. As a result, five years later, Judge Jeffreys arrested the host on a charge of treason and accepted payment of £15,000 to release him. In 1702 the estate came by marriage to Francis Gwyn, Secretary for War under Queen Anne, who presented to him a set of Mortlake tapestries from the Raphael cartoons now in the Victoria and Albert Museum. They hang today in the saloon. From 1815-18 Jeremy Bentham rented Forde, to the surprise of Sir Samuel Romilly, who felt the magnificence of the house inconsistent with the tenant's philosophy and mode of life. Since the house has changed only a little since Bentham's time we can still share Sir Samuel's astonishment.

The road from Maiden Newton to Crewkerne passes through no settlements at all for at least 12 miles, as it bears fairly straight (the hallmark of the turnpike roads) over the hills north of the Hooke valley and past Beaminster and Broadwindsor. Quite suddenly it drops past Wynyards Gap, Cheddington, where in a shrubby spot with a splendid view to east and north-west, stands the war memorial of the 43rd Wessex Regiment, a replica of that on a hill near Caen. Falling 500 feet in a mile and a half the road continues to the Somerset border at South Perrott, which bestrides the road with houses of golden stone and thatch, and a thirteenth-century church, south of which are undulations in a field—all that remains of a medieval castle.

North of the road in this far western corner of the county are a number of hamlets reached along narrow and winding lanes among hills lower and gentler than those further south and east. At Corscombe the moated manor, dating partly from about 1300 and clearly visible from the road, was purchased in 1741 by Thomas Hollis, a gentleman of unusual principles in his day. Having discovered entry to Parliament impossible without bribery, he began to collect books inimical to tyranny and dictatorship. Many of them he gave to learned libraries, including those of Berne, Zürich, and Harvard. Boswell described him as 'the strenuous Whig, who used to send over Europe presents of democratical books, with their boards stamped with daggers and caps of liberty', and it need not surprise anyone that Johnson's Tory circle disliked him. Having led the life of a recluse, (abstaining incidentally from alcohol, butter, milk, spices, and salt) he died at Corscombe in 1774 and by his own direction was buried in a field on his estate, without any mark to show his grave. Johnson's characterisation of him, 'A poor, dull creature as ever lived', seems one of the Great Cham's more reprehensible injustices.

Not far away, West Chelborough, at the end of a long cul-de-sac, has a small church with a little pinnacled tower of 1638. Its plain interior is relieved by a monument to a lady of the Kymer family who apparently died in childbirth. Her effigy lies in a recess. She is represented on her side in an awkward posture, her head thrown back, her neck displayed. She is swathed in bed-clothes, and the baby lies by her at the level of her hips. The group is simple and very moving.

East Chelborough consists of the manor farm and no more. Just south of it, on Castle Hill is said to be the site of a medieval castle, the bailey of which, on the north side, clutches an en-closure in two claw-like ramparts. The village church lies two miles off, hidden in a coppice in the grounds of Lewcomb House. Built in the eighteenth century it claims to be the sixth smallest parish church in England, and certainly a pair of cottages close by dwarfs it. Tradition says that it was intended to be built at East Chelborough, but every night the fairies removed to its present site what had been put up during the day. If anywhere one might believe such a story, here is the place.

CHAPTER FIVE

Dorchester and Central Dorset

As the county town of Dorset, Dorchester is the focal point of communications and government. It contains the county museum (a good one), stands on the longest of the rivers which flow from source to sea entirely in Dorset, and of the county's larger centres of population has the earliest origins. In size it takes third place, after Poole and Weymouth, but like them shows some of the less attractive symptoms of mid-twentieth century spreading.

The pattern of streets in the town centre suggests a Roman plan, but the proximity of the bivallate Iron Age camp at Poundbury (pronounced Pummery) to the immediate north-west proves if not occupation at least use of the site of Dorchester by the tribe whom the Romans conquered. A little while after the conquest they turned whatever settlement may have existed into a Roman town, which they called *Durnovaria*. In *The Mayor of Casterbridge* (his name for Dorchester) Hardy writes that it 'announced old Rome in every street, alley, and precinct', but he deliberately exaggerated. Years later he commented, 'When somebody said to me that "Casterbridge" is a sort of essence of the town as it used to be . . . I could not absolutely contradict him, though I could not quite perceive it'. Certainly, Roman remains appear often enough during building work inside the line of the walls. In 1936, a hoard of 22,000 coins, mostly dating from A.D. 200-257 was discovered in South Street, and during work on County Hall in Colliton Park several Roman buildings were unearthed. One of them remains to be seen in a sunken lawn in the grounds of County Hall, its flint rubble walls now a foot or two high, hypocausts and stokeholes open to the sun, the well a few yards away. A small column from the well has been somewhat incongruously placed on a wall of the house, and a wooden covering with a glass panel protects a geometrically patterned tessellated pavement.

Of other Roman buildings only mosaics are recorded, and some of them have been relaid in the County Museum in High West Street. A piece of Roman town wall, flint and limestone rubble bereft of its ashlar facing, stands in West Walk. The lines of the Roman walls, as far as they can be traced were laid out in the early eighteenth century with trees, and remain today as the Walks, elegant and formal, so that despite the antiquity of their origins they breathe an air of the less distant past. Indeed West and South Walks suggest a Victorian suburb. On their outer side they pass a park containing a small, blue-and-cream Victorian clock tower and a delicately ornate, oriental-flavoured band-stand in wrought iron with a pointed pagoda-type roof, while further on unmistakably Victorian town houses, solid and comfortable, are established on tree-lined avenues.

The west gate was probably at the end of High West Street, where it meets West Walk, the south gate near the junction of South Street and South Walk, the east gate by the junction of Salisbury Street and High East Street. We lose track of the wall here, but it probably followed the line of the Frome, to the northern boundary of Colliton Park, to turn sharply south again along The Grove. Several Roman cemeteries lie outside the perimeter, which encloses about 80 acres. Maumbury Rings, a little southward along the Weymouth road began as a neolithic henge monument, with its bank outside the ditch, but the Romans adapted it for use as an amphitheatre. It is about 115 yards in diameter overall, and its bank stands 20 to 30 feet high. It was used for most of the Roman period.

In later days it became the site of the gallows and 10,000 people gathered there in 1705 to watch the execution of a young woman. She was Mrs. Mary Channing, the daughter of a Dorchester merchant forced by her parents to marry a grocer. Having practically ruined her husband by her resentful extravagance she then poisoned him. After the trial her punishment was postponed because of her pregnancy, but 11 weeks after the birth of her child she was strangled and burnt as a public spectacle, in the fashion of the time. A century and a half later, when Hardy was still a child, his father took him to the same place to see the burning, this time only in effigy, of the Pope and Cardinal Wiseman during the No Popery riots.

Dorchester dwindled after the Romans left, and had no particular importance at the time of the Conquest, but the Normans built a castle there which has now vanished, and in 1364 a priory was founded, of which similarly no trace survives. During the later Middle Ages the town thrived, however, and by the seventeenth century was ready for its share of the disasters by fire that razed so many Dorset towns. In 1613, on Friday, 16 August, 300 houses and the churches of Holy Trinity and All Saints were burnt down in a holocaust which originated in the workshop of a tallow chandler who made his cauldron too hot and set the tallow alight. Somehow, the fire caused no deaths. Later fires, serious though less extensive, occurred: in 1622, caused by a maltster; 1725, started in a brewhouse; and 1775, when a soapboiler is blamed. On this last occasion thatched houses suffered badly, and one of the primitive fire-engines used at the time was itself destroyed.

As a result of all this devastation Dorchester has a distinctly nineteenth-century look, with a growing quantity of twentieth-century features. There are, however, some pleasant Georgian buildings, particularly at the western end of High West Street approaching Top o' Town. A teashop here claims to date from 1635. The Shire Hall, plain and decent, was rebuilt in 1796, and saw the trial of the Tolpuddle Martyrs. On the other side of the road is the seventeenth-century house with timber-framed windows and balcony, where Judge Jeffreys lodged when he conducted his infamous Assize after the defeat of Monmouth. It is now a restaurant, a little difficult despite its original ceiling beams and fireplaces to associate with the execution of 73 unfortunates and the exhibition of their heads, and quarters of their bodies, in towns and villages up and down Dorset and Somerset. 'Nappers Mite' in South Street, a group of shops and a restaurant in grey stone grouped round a little courtyard, was formerly almshouses founded in 1615 by Sir Robert Napier.

The only church to escape the fire of 1613, and the worst ravages of the nineteenth-century restorers, was St. Peter's, at the junction of South Street and the High Street at a point where its tower of almost white limestone, 90 feet high, with golden battlements and pinnacles, forms a visual climax from both east and south. The main fabric of the church dates from the fifteenth century. The south doorway is richly ornate transitional Norman, the pulpit (entered by the stairs which once led to the rood loft) Jacobean. The whole has an air of antiquity, of the continuity of past and present. West of the south door can be found a memorial to Thomas Hardy, of Melcombe Regis, a common ancestor of the admiral and the novelist, and founder of the local grammar school. The west end of the north aisle is plethoric with a huge baroque monument to Denzil Holles, one of Charles I's 'Five Members', and one of the two who held the Speaker in the chair when he refused in 1628 to put Sir John Eliot's Remonstrance, Holles reclines as at supper in Roman military dress but for his restoration periwig, while *putti* justifiably weep below.

Dorchester as a whole supported the Parliamentary cause vehemently, and Holles' monument is therefore aptly housed, though it may be noted that as a moderate he came to disapprove of Cromwell and his policies and not only suffered a period of exile as a result, but served Charles II after the Restoration. Trinity Church, a few yards away, has a memorial of nineteenth-century origin to John White, another moderate Puritan, and rector of that church from 1606. Fuller described him as 'A grave

man, yet without moroseness . . . by whose wisdom the town of Dorchester . . . was much enriched'. White was an outstanding preacher who, again to quote Fuller, 'absolutely commanded his own passions and the purses of his parishioners, whom he could wind up to what height he pleased on important occasions'. His lasting achievement was the promotion of the colonisation of Massachusetts, and thanks partly to his advocacy a Dorset ship under the command of John Endicott, a Dorchester man, set out from Weymouth in 1628 for Cape Ann. In the following year a royal charter was granted, and Endicott became the first Governor.

The town's intimate association with the two literary giants of Dorset, Hardy and William Barnes, is decently commemorated by two unpretentious statues, that to Barnes outside St. Peter's, and that to Hardy (by Eric Kennington) at Top o' Town, where he sits pensively contemplating the Military Museum.

Though neither was born in Dorchester, both spent long periods of their lives working here or not far away. Hardy went to school here from the age of nine, and at 16, in 1856, was apprenticed to John Hicks, an architect, who practised in South Street. Here, by great good fortune, literature, especially the Classics, seem to have occupied everyone's time almost as much as architecture, for Hicks himself was something of a scholar, and a fellow pupil of Hardy's was well grounded in Latin and Greek. It so happened that William Barnes kept a school next door (really an astonishing coincidence) and when disputes on grammatical matters arose Hardy would call on him to settle them.

Barnes was born near Sturminster Newton in 1801, and his formal education finished at the age of 13, so that he was virtually self-educated. Having worked in Dorchester as a solicitor's clerk from 1818-23, he moved to Mere, in Wiltshire, where he opened a school. During his stay there he extended his studies from Latin and Greek to French, German, Italian, and Persian. He practised

21 *Dorchester, looking down the High Street, with St. Peter's Parish Church on the left*

wood-engraving ('quickened', he wrote, '. . . by Bewick's works'), and in 1828 made enquiries as to the possibility of working for Rudolf Ackermann. He played the flute, piano, and violin, he sang and composed, he began a diary in Italian, studied Welsh poetry, and—most significant—started writing poems in Dorset dialect. In 1827 he married Julia Miles, the daughter of a Dorchester Excise man, and eight years later returned to the town to keep a school first in Durngate Street then in South Street, in a house next to Nappers's Mite. A third move, to the other side of the road, brought him as we have seen next door to Hicks.

He was a gentle person, who kept order in school without using the cane, but suffered in material matters from his modesty and refusal to regard his own abilities as exceptional. In the long run his school failed to prosper, and towards the end of his stay in Dorchester he experienced penury. The death of his wife in 1852 was a severe blow, and for the next ten years little went right for him. His school had virtually run down when, in 1862 he not only gained the incumbency of Whitcombe and Winterborne Came, but thanks to the efforts of Coventry Patmore a Civil List pension. He died in 1886, still mourning his beloved Julia, but at least not without creature comforts.

People recalled him in Dorchester looking much like his statue, white-bearded and bald, wearing silver-buckled shoes, unconventional hats, and a coat like the mongrel issue of a cassock and a dressing gown. Scholars remembered him for his philological work, particularly his desire to purify English of Latinisms and to substitute, for example, 'foresay' for preface, 'push-wainling' for perambulator, and 'wire-spell' for telegram. The rest of us ought to remember him for his poetry. Ought to—but rarely do. Had he written in the dialect not of Dorset but of Lowland Scotland, his fame might have rivalled that of the near-namesake with whom he is sometimes compared. Indeed, the Scots overrate Burns as perversely as the English neglect and underestimate Barnes.

The suburb of Fordington, to the south-east of the town and by the Frome, was a separate manor in the Doomsday Survey, where it belonged to the King (like Dorchester itself). Later it became part of the estate of the Duchy of Cornwall. In Hutchins' day it was known as Icen Town, possibly a corruption of Eastern Town, and still has a street called Icen Way. Its church, St. George's, overlooks a triangular green, flanked on its second side by mean Victorian, on its third by satisfying Georgian housing. It is a long building of grey stone with dressings of Ham Hill stone, and a particularly handsome fifteenth-century tower. The Norman tympanum over the south door bears a curious carving said to represent St. George aiding the Crusaders at the battle of Dorylaeum, and according to a tradition the stones forming the base of the second Norman column in the south arcade came from the church of St. George's burial in Lydda. An early twentieth-century vicar seems to have been obsessed with restoring the church to its medieval condition, to which end he enlarged and heightened the nave and replaced a Georgian chancel with a longer one in Gothic, despite the opposition of his distinguished parishioner, Thomas Hardy. The total effect is now admittedly spacious, even monumental, but untidy. A Roman tombstone of the first century A.D., the only inscribed one ever found in Dorset, was uncovered when the floor of the church was being lowered, and rests now against the wall at the west end of the nave.

Two miles south-west of Dorchester a great hump of a hill, surrounded near its long summit by a multiple ring of enormous ramparts, glowers across the plain at the rising flood of modern houses which threatens to engulf the green fields. This is Maiden Castle, the encampment of Mai Dun, the Fortress by the Plain. The enclosed area covers about 1200 acres, and no hill fort in Dorset surpasses it in size. Its outer perimeter measures two miles, it is 1000 yards long, and 500 wide, and its ramparts are 60 feet high, protecting the two entrances in an intricate system of overlapping, so that attackers might be subjected to prolonged attack with sling and bow from their flanks.

Excavation before the last war showed that its history goes back to about 2000 B.C., when a Neolithic village covering ten to fifteen acres was established on the eastern part. Later on a bank barrow was raised about a third of a mile long, but today not visible, and a young man killed, dismembered, and buried at its eastern end. His brain and pieces of his skull had been removed before inhumation, perhaps for purposes of ritual cannibalism. The settlement underwent conquest by an invading tribe in the middle of the second millennium B.C. then was deserted for a thousand years.

About 300 B.C. Iron Age people re-occupied the site of the neolithic settlement and fortified it, built huts and storage pits, and laid out streets, over an area of 45 acres. Two centuries later the triple rampart was built, stone platforms now buried established as vantage points for the defenders of those lethally elaborate entrances, hordes of slingstones deposited nearby, and walls of limestone blocks set up on either side of the main gateway. Fifty years before the Roman conquest the Durotriges, as the Romans called the inhabitants of this part of the country, refurbished their defences and re-metalled some of the streets.

In A.D. 43 the Romans came. The conquest of the south-west was entrusted to the Second Augustan Legion, under the officer destined to become the Emperor Vespasian. His troops stormed and took Maiden Castle after a bitter battle, of whose relics some can be seen in the County Museum. One skeleton still has an arrow-head lodged in the spine. Occupation of Maiden Castle continued until about A.D. 70, when the inhabitants were probably moved into the Roman town of *Durnovaria*. But three centuries later, at the end of the Roman occupation, a pagan temple was established to an unknown god by the eastern entrance, and a two-roomed house built for a priest. Since then, the great fortress has lain unused, except for grazing, brooding over the countryside like the shade of an old menace.

On its southern side a little stream known as the South Winterborne to distinguish it from another Winterborne in the centre of the county, flows past from Winterborne Abbas eastward, to join the Frome near West Stafford. Five settlements on its banks bear its name and two others used to. Just west of Winterborne Abbas on the Dorchester-Bridport road the Nine Stones, a small circle, 25 feet wide, of rough megaliths dating from about 1500 B.C. stands in the shade of a mature and splendid beech tree, which lends an appropriately magical atmosphere to the site. Winterborne Steepleton, crowded on either side by wooded hills, has a church with one of the three medieval spires in Dorset (the others are at Trent and Iwerne Minster). Though a fragment of carving built into the north wall, representing a flying angel, dates back possibly to the eighth century, most of the church is fifteenth century, like the spire. Winterborne Monkton huddles in the shadow of Maiden Castle, a scatter of ugly houses quite unworthy of that stupendous work, though its odd little church, which has a south arcade of three asymmetrical arches, should be visited for an unexpectedly moving late Victorian effigy of a young girl with long, flowing tresses. She was a Williams, of the family that lived at Herringston, the next Winterborne village, where only the Jacobean manor house now remains.

Once past Maiden Castle the valley opens out. The hills are lower, the slopes gentler, the valley floor broader and flatter. Winterborne Came has Came House (1754), a handsome Palladian design, on a perfect site on the southern slope of the valley. Next to it, hidden in a wood, isolated, and retired, stands Barnes' church, built of grey ashlar, but on the north side subtly coloured with lichen of orange, claret, and the palest blue-green. The interior has a sixteenth-century rood screen, a Jacobean pulpit, an altar tomb of the same period with effigies of an intelligent-looking, sharp-nosed man and woman, and another altar tomb with brasses. Barnes is buried in the churchyard. His thatched and colour-washed rectory stands by the Dorchester-Wareham road, over the brow of the hill towards Dorchester. Whitcombe church, the oversight of which he combined with Came, rests in a field half a mile nearer Wareham, deliberately kept more or less as it was in his day, lighted by oil lamps. It has chancel, nave, and tower of the twelfth to fifteenth centuries, some fragments of a Saxon cross, medieval wall painting, and a mossy, undulating roof.

Broadmayne, further south-east, has little to recommend it, but the reminiscence of Hardy's father that there 'three wooden-legged men danced a three-handed reel'. Two miles to the west of it, on the hills overlooking Sutton Poyntz and Preston, are two notable barrow groups, including a bank barrow, with a splendid view of Portland looking like a Dreadnought of 1914. North from Broadmayne, the church at West Knighton is worth a pause, while West Stafford rates a thorough look. The village street winds among brick, stone, and thatch. The church, which was largely rebuilt in 1640, has its original screen and pulpit (with tester), some Jacobean pews, and the Royal Arms of James I. There are monuments from the late sixteenth to the eighteenth century, and a quite horrible Victorian tomb with a cadaver in alabaster.

Woodsford Castle, two miles and a half down the Frome, became a farm-house in the eighteenth century, with an enormous thatched roof, but it dates back to 1337, when a certain William de Whitefield was given leave to crenellate his manor house at 'Wyrdesford'. Though it still has walls five and a half feet thick, with arrow slits, it looks anything but warlike, but its age places it with Godlingston, Barnston, and Owermoigne, as one of the four oldest inhabited buildings in the county.

Across the Frome and nearer Dorchester we are in Hardy country with a vengeance. Stinsford is Mellstock in *Under the Greenwood Tree*, and its church was the parish church of Hardy's parents. His birthplace, at Higher Bockhampton, still secluded, and best approached on foot from the south through a wood of beech and chestnut (carefully signposted from the car park) is now owned by the National Trust. His heart lies in Stinsford churchyard, where other Hardys are buried, including both his wives.

The church itself is pleasant, but remarkable mainly for its associations. Apart from the Hardy graves and connections it harbours the remains of Lady Susan Fox-Strangways and her husband, the actor and dramatist, William O'Brien. They married clandestinely in 1764, to the horror of aristocratic society, expressed by Walpole, who wrote; 'Even a footman were preferable. I could not have believed that Lady Susan would have stooped so low'. The bride's father, Lord Ilchester, insisted on O'Brien's leaving the stage, and so cut short a promising career. The marriage appears despite the social difficulties to have been a success.

In contrast to the flat country of the lower Frome valley, west and north-west of Dorchester the land becomes hilly, and river valleys narrower. The main roads to Sherborne and to Crewkerne (the latter as far as Maiden Newton) both run for a great part of the way along the valleys, but the Yeovil and Bridport roads, which partly follow the routes of Roman roads or, like the alternative route to Sherborne through Charminster, date from the turnpike era, lead nonchalantly over the hills.

The main route up the Frome valley on the north bank is duplicated on the south side by a narrow lane which the Romans used, skirting the southern ramparts of Poundbury and the remnants of the aqueduct by which they brought water into *Durnovaria* with a head of pressure for ease of distribution. It continues through the grey village of Bradford Peverell, but peters out as a practical route for cars beyond the hamlet of Muckleford a mile further on.

On the main road the first village, Stratton, has a church with a sixteenth-century timber staircase in the tower, enclosed in an oak case with linenfold panelling and supported on a stem like a contemporary pulpit. A mile past it the Crewkerne road moves off to the left, and the Yeovil route soars up over the downs to drive through to its destination outside the county uninterrupted by any village or hamlet. Towards its northern end as it descends Bubb Down Hill a winding road to the left meanders through tree-shaded pasture-land to Melbury House, which, with the parish church, is all that remains of the village of Melbury Sampford. In the early Middle Ages it belonged to the ubiquitous Turberviles, passing to the Sampford family, probably in the thirteenth century. Marriage brought it the Brownings who held it until the reign of Henry VII, when Henry Strangways bought it for 600 marks (£400). It was his son Giles who purchased the site of the monastery at Abbotsbury and to whom much of Melbury as it is today must be attributed. When Leland visited him in 1540 he had already built the hexagonal tower and much besides, using 3000 loads of Ham Hill stone. The east front was remodelled in 1692 and repairs and alterations in the following two centuries give a misleading idea of the bulding's age. The setting of the house, facing a small valley filled with a lake, suggests sheer spaciousness, which the careful landscaping emphasises. Inside are some good ceilings and paintings, an excellent set of Mortlake tapestries, sixteenth-century panelling, and some delicate and fine wood carvings of fruit, birds, and musical instruments ascribed to Grinling Gibbons.

The interior of the little church is quite overwhelmed by the profusion of ostentatious Fox-Strangways monuments in marble. There are two fifteenth-century altar tombs, both of Purbeck marble with alabaster effigies, and both originally commemorating members of the Browning family. One was appropriated for the acquisitive Sir Giles Strangways, who died in 1547. His son and namesake has a brass on the west wall of the south transept.

North of Melbury Sampford, and like it, off the main road,

Melbury Osmund lies crocked in a green, benign valley, and largely on a cul-de-sac which leads to a northern entrance to Melbury Park, after crossing a little stream by a watersplash at the valley bottom. Its houses are largely stone and thatch, among trees felicitously placed to make pictures. The church, which was built in 1745 and refurbished in 1888, incorporates in the north wall of the chancel a tenth century carving of a frog-like creature entangled with foliage or vines.

Having parted from the Yeovil road, the road up the Frome valley continues along the river's left bank as far as Maiden Newton. On the way it runs through Frampton, which used to be the seat of a family called Browne. Having bought it from Sir Christopher Hatton during the reign of Elizabeth, they held it until 1833, when the last male Browne left it to his brother-in-law, a distinguished soldier, Sir Colquhoun Grant. As a Major-General he commanded a brigade at Waterloo, where he lost five horses in the fighting. His daughter, who inherited, married a grandson of the playwright Sheridan. Frampton Court, built by a Browne in 1705, was pulled down in 1935. In 1844, Sheridan invited William Barnes to visit him here to meet his gifted sisters, Caroline Norton, and Lady Dufferin, who had admired poems Barnes had published in the *Dorset County Chronicle*. Although he at first refused 'on the grounds that he was unaccustomed to society', the poet finally yielded, and made a friend of Mrs. Norton, who for some years was the only writer of any importance to appreciate his work. The church contains some fifteenth-century remnants almost obliterated by the Victorians, but its tower, dating from 1695, is unusual in having Tuscan columns for angle buttresses. The north aisle and chancel display a profusion of Browne monuments.

At Maiden Newton the Hooke river finishes its journey through the Tollers to flow into the Frome. The church has some architecture of every century from the twelfth to the sixteenth, the roof of the nave—restored in 1940, of all times—dating from the

23 *Early spring sunshine in Sydling St. Nicholas*

fifteenth. The village itself can offer little but second-class Victoriana, and some dull earlier bits and pieces.

The country southwards is the continuation to the east of the majestic downland culminating in Eggardon. It lacks population and roads, and such settlements as it holds are small, remote, and concealed in hollows out of reach of the worst of the winds that drive the rain over the hill-tops and the broad fields. One of these settlements, Wynford Eagle, has a manor house of grey stone in a wide, walled garden by a road junction. Its roof has red tiles, and its windows mullions of golden stone, and on a gable high on its west front perches a great stone eagle glaring into the setting sun.

This carving and the second element in the name commemorate the early connection of the manor with the honour of the Eagle, the possessions of the Norman baron, Gilbert de Aquila, of Pevensey, in Sussex. By the mid-fifteenth century the manor had come by purchase to the Sydenham family, which had its hour of glory 200 years later. The Sydenhams declared for Parliament, and at least four of five Sydenham brothers fought the King. One of them, William, commanded the Parliamentary forces in Dorset, and was one of the founder members of the Protectorate, and a member of Cromwell's Council. His brother, Thomas (born in 1624), became a physician in practice at Cambridge, earning a place of honour in the history of medicine, and the distrust of his colleagues, by basing his treatment not on dogma but on careful observation of his patients. He has been called the 'English Hippocrates' and the founder of clinical medicine.

The end of the family in the next generation was a comedy with a tragic denouement. Another William Sydenham was Squire of the Body to William III ('and the last', Hutchins observes, 'to hold that office'). He put up his estate in a private lottery, having somehow arranged that the winning ticket should be held by a young lady relative who was to sell back her winnings cheaply. Unfortunately for him the scheme miscarried. The winner refused to sell, but got married and brought Wynford Eagle to her husband, so that Sydenham, outraged, found himself estateless. He and his two daughters compounded their folly by refusing to hand over the property and ended their days in Dorchester gaol.

The main road leaves the river at Maiden Newton, but up the narrowing valley of the Frome are several villages attractive by their remoteness as much as for any other reason. Chilfrome sits hidden among trees. Cattistock is a village almost entirely of the nineteenth century, and so is its church tower, which in 1940 lost by fire its carillon of 35 bells, but remains tall and graceful, its vertical lines finely emphasised by its high and narrow belfry windows. The ground stage of the tower is used as a baptistry, lavishly decorated, and provided with a fantasy of a font cover, carved with gothic elaboration and all of 20 feet high. Some little way to the west the small twelfth- and thirteenth-century church at Wraxhall has a monument to William Laurence, who died in 1682. He was a Scottish judge, and in 1680 published a treatise on marriage which he is said to have written 'on a discontent with his wife (a red-haired, buxom woman) whom he suspected of dishonesty'.

Frome St. Quentin is a bright little village, not far from which lies the poetically named old house of Chantmarle, so called from the family which owned the estate in the later Middle Ages. Its attractive east front of golden stone has a slim oriel window corbelled out over the porch, and looks early sixteenth century, though in fact it was built in an old-fashioned style about 1612, while the west wing dates from the fifteenth century. It is now a police training centre.

The Frome rises at Evershot, which is otherwise distinguished for the bow windows in its main street, and the brass dated 1520 in the much restored church, depicting the Rector, William Grey, celebrating Mass in pre-Reformation vestments. West of the Frome and north of Dorchester the drainage of the central chalk mass of the county runs north and south, and consequently so do most of the roads. Tracks, footpaths, and a few narrow country roads cross or link them, but generally speaking travel northward or southward is easier than eastward or westward until the chalk is crossed and its northern escarpment descended into Blackmore Vale.

Between Stratton and Frampton one of the chalk streams, the Sydling Water, flows into the Frome, and as the main road rises, wooded, to the hill top, a side turning runs under the railway into a suddenly different landscape, a gentle valley with space for the rivulet to meander past water meadows and watercress beds. At Sydling St. Nicholas, a typical valley village, long and narrow, streams gush along and under the streets, past thatched cottages of stone and flint bands. The church, bristling luxuriantly with fearsome gargoyles, is full of personality, and despite a Victorian restoration blends piquantly the fifteenth with the eighteenth century. Nearby a sixteenth-century barn, again of stone and flint, has elaborate roof-timbers supported by thick oak posts, though the roof itself is of corrugated iron. One of the beams is supposed to have been carved with the initials and date L V W 1590, for Lady Ursula Walsingham, the estate at that time being owned by Sir Francis Walsingham, Elizabeth's brilliant chief of intelligence.

Along the next valley runs the main road from Dorchester to Sherborne, by the side of the river Cerne. Its confluence with the Frome is just outside Dorchester at Charminster (originally Cerne Minster, of course), an ordinarily pretty village with an outstanding church which manages to combine impressions of solidity and spaciousness. Largely of the twelfth century, it has a Norman chancel arch and two Transitional arcades of high quality. Just as the Turbeviles left their mark at Bere Regis, and the Brownes at Frampton, so Charminster bears the impress of a local family, in this instance the Trenchards. A wall monument with a kneeling effigy commemorates Grace Pole, a Trenchard daughter, who died in 1638, and two earlier altar tombs lacking inscriptions or effigies and robbed of their brasses, are assumed to belong to other Trenchards. The church tower, with its Ham stone dressings, bears on its buttresses a distinctive monogram of Sir Thomas Trenchard, who built it early in the sixteenth century.

The family lived at their manor house, Wolfeton, not far away, having obtained it by marriage in 1480. During the following century they built there extensively, but what remains is a fragment of their work. The gatehouse, curiously asymmetrical, its south tower larger than the north (both provided with arrow slits) is probably in part earlier than the rest. It contains a spiral staircase with steps hewn from solid oak, each with a rounded end that overlaps the one below, so dispensing with a newel.

In January, 1506, the Archduke Philip of Austria and his Spanish wife, Joanna, on their way from the Netherlands to Spain were caught in rough weather and forced to put in at Weymouth. They were brought to Wolfeton (an indication of the importance of the Trenchards at that time) and their host, Sir Thomas Trenchard, sent for his travelled kinsman, John Russell, of Berwick, near Bridport, to act as interpreter. A highly personable young man, he accompanied Philip and Joanna to the court at Windsor, whither they went at King Henry's command or invitation. Russell made himself so useful and agreeable there that he stayed at Court after the departure of the Austrian couple, becoming ultimately Duke of Bedford, and founding a line that has produced its full share of statesmen and individualists. An enormous oak chimney piece, carved with columns, entablature, panels, figures, and enrichments, and dominating the drawing room at Wolfeton, is reputed to have been given to Sir Thomas Trenchard by his royal guests in gratitude for his hospitality. More probably, however, it dates from a hundred years after their departure, despite the early Tudor carvings, which appear to have been inserted, round the fireplace. On at least two known occasions Wolfeton was visited by Sir Walter Raleigh, while he lived at Sherborne. That Churchillian figure, soldier, statesman, and man of letters, with so much of the brilliance and weakness of Winston Churchill, the same capacity for leadership and for making enemies, the same boldness sometimes amounting to rashness, the same fundamental humanity, found himself under suspicion of atheism. An account was given to a commission of enquiry at Cerne Abbas of a supper party given at Wolfeton in 1593 by Sir George Trenchard, attended by Raleigh and other guests including two Puritan ministers. He became involved in a discussion with these two on the nature of the deity, in which the Calvinists used a circular argument of no appeal to Raleigh's clear mind. He ended it by asking impatiently for grace to be said, 'For', he observed, 'that is better than this disputation.' Later in the same year Sir George Trenchard, as Deputy Lieutenant, had arrested a Jesuit priest, John Cornelius, at Chideock Castle, the home of the catholic Arundels, and on instructions from the Privy Council had him confronted at Wolfeton with anti-Catholic clergymen, including one of the Calvinists with whom Raleigh had argued. Raleigh himself was again present and in due course took over the disputation, which he and Cornelius continued alone until dawn. Although Raleigh promised to intercede for him, there is no evidence that he did, and the priest was executed at Dorchester.

The next village upstream is Godmanston, where the Smith's Arms claims to be the smallest public house in England, and the church has features from the twelfth to the fifteenth centuries. At Nether Cerne manor house and church nestle together at the end of a muddy cul-de-sac, an architectural sonata in stone and flint.

Cerne Abbas, two miles upstream, is a picture-book village,

hemmed in by the downs and full of history and tradition. Its profusion of Georgian and seventeenth-century buildings, the row of fifteenth-century houses in Abbey Street, and the handsome church tower, lend it great distinction of themselves, even without taking into account the somewhat exiguous ruins of the abbey, the enigmatic figure cut in the turf of Giant's Hill, and the profusion of prehistoric remains on the green downs round about.

Medieval tradition recorded by William of Malmesbury attributes the founding of the Abbey to St. Augustine, at whose command the spring still to be seen in the old churchyard gushed up to enable him to baptise the local inhabitants. The first firm information of a religious house here, however, comes much later. Edwold, the brother of King Edmund of East Anglia, who was murdered by the Danes, is said to have declined the crown and retired as a hermit 'near a spring called the Silver Well, which St. Austin produced at Cerne'. He died and was buried there in 871, but a century later his bones were transferred to the church built on the site of the present parish church, when Ethelmar, Earl of Cornwall, endowed a monastery at Cerne, completing it in 987.

The first Abbot, Aelfric, was a scholar, sent to the new foundation to set it on the right path, and translator of his own homilies into Anglo-Saxon for the sake of his ignorant monks. He went from Cerne to St. Albans, and from 994 until his death in 1005 held the Archbishopric of Canterbury. Margaret of Anjou stayed here for a short time in 1471 on her way to defeat at Tewkesbury, and the later Cardinal Morton was a monk here.

Little enough remains of the Abbey buildings. The porch of the Abbot's Hall, a three-storeyed tower with a fine oriel window, reminiscent of the contemporary gateway at Forde, stands isolated in the garden of Abbey House, which itself, though rebuilt in the eighteenth century, incorporates a fragment of what may have been the Abbey gatehouse. A separate building in the grounds was probably the Abbot's lodging, while the fourteenth-century tithe barn, in the south-west of the village, is now much altered and adapted as dwelling houses. North of the churchyard is a set of banks and ditches forming enclosures, within which are three circular mounds of unexplained significance. Lastly, of course, as at Wool, Abbotsbury and almost everywhere else where a monastery was destroyed after the Dissolution, buildings in the village often incorporate pieces of carved stone filched centuries ago from the ruins.

The graceful church tower, a carving of the Madonna and Child in a niche on its west front, has already been mentioned. The rest of the church is worthy of it. A light and spacious Perpendicular building, it has a thirteenth-century chancel with remnants of medieval wall painting, including a vigorous picture of the beheading of John the Baptist. Its rood screen of stone dates from the fifteenth century, and the pulpit, complete with tester, from 1640.

So obviously prosperous and cared for is Cerne Abbas today that Treves' description in 1906 comes as a shock. 'It is silent and well-nigh deserted', he wrote. 'Sad to tell, Cerne Abbas is dying and has already fallen into a state of hebetude.' One hopes that his prognoses as a surgeon were better than this. The village is very much alive, and looks it. Though it has not escaped some insensitive building it remains one of the most attractive places in Dorset, and has an organic unity, a fortuitous harmony, like that of the countryside in which it is set.

Oddly enough even the Giant was almost invisible in Treves' day, though fortunately he is now in the care of the National Trust and kept clearly in view. On the western slope of the hill north of the village he is cut in outline, with a few anatomical details—eyebrows, eyes, nose and mouth, nipples, ribs, and ithyphallic genitalia. He brandishes a club in his right hand. Above him is a curious rectangular earthwork called the Trendle,

or the Frying Pan, where until the turn of the century folk danced round a maypole on May Day. Statistics convey something of the Giant's impressiveness, for he is 60 yards tall, his club measures 40 yards, his phallus 10 yards, and his shoulders are 15 yards across.

The figure's origins are problematic. According to one story it commemorated a giant who feasted on sheep and was killed by 'enraged peasants' as he slept. Another tale held that it was cut at the Dissolution of the Monasteries, to ridicule the Abbot, the obvious masculinity representing his lust, the club his desire for revenge, and the position of his feet enforced departure. This theory may have some connection with the accusation brought in 1535 by one of the monks that the last Abbot kept concubines, spent the abbey's funds on his progeny and accosted women in the streets.

The view generally accepted today is that the Giant dated from the time of the Emperor Commodus, who in A.D. 191 proclaimed himself an incarnation of Hercules. The associations of that god with fertility allowed his representation in aggressively masculine form, and possibly enabled the local Romano-British to identify him with the god of a local cult. Walter of Coventry, writing about 1230, says there was a local deity called Helith, which as Helis or Heil occurs in the later literature. The Giant used reputedly to drink at the river after sunset to catch and eat virgins, and sexual intercourse on his body was supposed to cure barrenness or sterility. The maypole, moreover, was originally a symbolic phallus, so the dancing on the Trendle probably had some connection with the rites of Helis Hercules. If in fact the Giant was a pre-Christian fertility god his persistence through the centuries despite the inhibiting presence of the monks just below him speaks volumes for the vigour of the old cult, for scouring of the figure must have taken place repeatedly. According to Hutchins the villagers undertook it every seven years—a suspiciously magical number—and the festivity which accompanied the scour-

25 *Athelhampton House, the Great Hall*

ings caused a nineteenth-century vicar to stop them, as encouraging immorality among the people. The St. Augustine legend moreover provides additional evidence of the power that Helis wielded over his people, for when the saint arrived on his evangelising errand the people of Cerne received him and his companions at first wth uncouth hostility, a tradition which suggests that the advance of Christianity here met with unusual resistance. It is easy enough to imagine that the commission of enquiry into Raleigh's alleged atheism might have felt as they deliberated in the house now called Barnwells, in Abbey Street, that in Cerne Abbas they had found an appropriate place to investigate the ungodly. To a modern eye the prehistoric settlement sites, field systems, and barrows, which mark the hills round about in such profusion, harmonise with the great idol's primitive origins and associations.

In the seventeenth century, Minterne Magna, north of Cerne, was a seat of the Churchill family, who hailed from Wootton Glanville in Blackmore Vale. The brother of the first Duke of Marlborough inherited it, and is remembered by a flamboyant monument in the church, recording his advancement in the royal service and his military prowess, for he 'was esteem'd one of the best Commanders of Foot in Europe'. He died in 1714, and his widow bequeathed the property out of the family.

We are almost on the edge of the chalk here, and from High Stoy, just to the north, off the main road, westward to Bubb Down Hill the escarpment is steep and impressive, with famous views northward from its top. The hamlet of Batcombe, now little more than the church, stands half way down the sharp slope enfolded by Batcombe Hill on a narrow, erratically winding lane. The story goes that a certain local squire, John Minterne, known as 'Conjuring Minterne' because he was held to be in league with the Devil, leaping on his horse from the crest of the hill into the village, knocked a pinnacle off the church tower. On the winding ridge above, just by the road which follows the hill-top, is the little stone pillar called Cross-in-Hand, whose origin and purpose are utterly mysterious, and which has attracted a quantity of legend and folklore. Hardy used two of the stories connected with it, one in *Tess*, the other in a poem, *The Lost Pyx*. Nothing in fact is known of it, and speculation may continue unfettered.

The Cerne is the last of the Frome's northern tributaries. The next valley belongs to the Piddle, which Victorian reticence called the Puddle or Trent, and which gives its older name to so many villages. Some of them we have seen in Chapter three, but Tolpuddle, Puddletown, Piddlehinton, and Piddletrenthide remain. The last two, stretched painfully along the valley, which scenically compares well with that of Cerne, are practically continuous, and rather dull, except for their churches. That at Piddletrenthide has a particularly fine tower, crenellated, and gargoyled, with lively animal carvings on the outside of the south aisle. Inside, the arcades are fifteenth century, the chancel arch has Norman responds, and the wall monuments are elegant. Piddlehinton has some fair brasses, and in the south transept a board telling us: 'A peal was rung at Piddlehinton Christmas Day Morning 1820 four hours and two minutes by Samuel Nelson, Robert Biles, William Old, Timothy Nelson, Adam Nelson'. At Alton St. Pancras, the most northerly village in the valley, the church lies off the main road between two large Georgian houses. It is largely Victorian but has two modern stained-glass windows, a mild one of 1956 at the west end, and a restrained but powerful and impressive design of 1964 in blues, purples, and red, in the north wall.

Puddletown, on the main road eastward out of Dorchester, presents a disheartening and unattractive face to the traffic rumbling through, but has a core of harmonious older buildings to be found if you are in no hurry. The church should on no account be missed. It is mainly Perpendicular, with a timber roof of the fifteenth century (restored, but tactfully), box pews, a possibly pre-Conquest font with a seventeenth-century cover, and a Jacobean pulpit. The minstrel's gallery, where Hardy's grandfather played the bass viol as a young man, bears the date 1635, and the Latin inscription, 'You have come here not to be seen, but to hear and pray'. On the south side of the nave, entered by an arch with panelled soffit and responds, is the so-called Athelhampton chantry, containing the tombs of the Martyn family. Altar tombs and effigies from the thirteenth to the fifteenth centuries lie here in great profusion, with two notable brasses. On one, Christopher Martyn (who died in 1524) kneels bareheaded before his Maker above this verse:

> *Here lyethe the body of Xpofer Martyn Esquyer*
>   *Sone and heire unto Syr Willyam Martyn, knyght,*
> *Praye for there Soules with hearty desyre*
>   *That they both may be heirs of Eternall Lyght*
> *Calling to remembrance that every Wyght*
>   *Most nedys dye, and therefor lett us pray,*
> *As other for us may do Another day.*

The other brass is of Nicholas Martyn, the last of the family, who died in 1595 leaving four daughters. His epitaph is said to have ended:

> *Nicholas the first, Martyn the last*
> *Good night, Nicholas.*

Regrettably, no trace remains of this.

The Martyns lived at Athelhampton, whence the name given to their chantry. It is still there, by the main road, from which it is shielded by trees, all in grey stone with a handsome oriel, crenellations, gables and chained apes. The latter were the family symbol, Martyn in medieval folklore being the name of the monkey, as Reynard was of the fox. The curious family motto, 'He who looks at Martyn's ape, Martyn's ape shall look at him', suggests an endearingly unheroic situation with comic undertones, though nothing in the records indicates that the Martyns lacked courage or resolution. The house now has lost much of what Nicholas Martyn bequeathed to his daughters, but what remains is fine enough, especially the great hall and its gallery and open timber roof, which dates from the late fifteenth century. The house and gardens are frequently open to the public during the summer.

The Martyns settled originally at Waterston, two miles nearer Piddlehinton, before obtaining Athelhampton by marriage in the reign of Edward III. Their earliest seat descended by marriage through several families until it came to the Howards of Bindon in the time of Elizabeth. Thomas, the third Lord Howard, who was responsible for much of Lulworth Castle, seems also to have built the manor house at Waterston, which finally Sir John Strangways bought in 1641. As it was it served Hardy as the model for Bathsheba Everdene's farmhouse in *Far From the Madding Crowd*, but suffered a disastrous fire in 1863, with the result that little of the interior is original.

The remaining village on the Piddle, Tolpuddle, has its own modest Jacobean manor, but its fame derives from that disgraceful episode in 1834 when local landlords led by the magistrate, James Frampton of Moreton, with the full support of Melbourne's government, used their power and privileges to crush an incipient association of farm labourers by means of a legal trick. The six instigators of the movement were sentenced to deportation for life, though thanks to public agitation they were brought back to England two years later, and have gone down to history as the Tolpuddle Martyrs. The sycamore tree under which they took their oath of membership, now hollow, stunted, and dying, bears no plaque or notice, although it is in the care of the National Trust.

At Puddletown the main roads from Dorchester separate, the northern turning leading to Blandford. At the first village on this road Milborne St. Andrew, a largely modern settlement now, the south doorway of the church is a brilliant Norman arrangement with double chevron ornamentation and voussoirs alternately in grey and yellow-orange stone. Not far off, over a hill, in the church at Dewlish, another doorway in precisely the same style, though smaller, is to be seen at the west end of the nave. This village has several houses of seventeenth-century date in flint, with stone or brick, while Dewlish House, a mile or so away in a lower lying park, is a good example of Queen Anne country-house architecture. It was built about 1702 for the son of a London merchant, and sold in the middle of the century to a Michel. His descendants developed a military tradition here, one becoming a General, and one, to whom a huge and hideous monument was set up in Dewlish church, a Field Marshal.

Roads north and north-west lead us into sparsely populated downland, a lonely landscape of grandeur without severity. At Cheselbourne, a straggling, untidy village, the church has a graceful tower and a hammer-beam roof. Bingham's Melcombe, now just the manor house and the church, hides itself in a shallow valley at the end of an avenue of elms, which leads to the medieval gatehouse. It was originally another Turbervile seat, which coming to the Binghams by marriage in the thirteenth century, acquired their name with them. The most illustrious Bingham, Sir Robert, fought at the battle of Lepanto, and served as governor of Connaught during Elizabeth's Irish wars. Although he gained a poor reputation for severity in that office (the name is still unloved in Ireland) he was a friend of Walsingham's, and seems to have shown talent as a soldier. He died in Dublin in 1598. Melcombe had been inherited by his brother, whose great-grandson was Parliamentary governor of Poole and commander at the final siege of Corfe Castle. The house, indeed, served as the Parliamentary headquarters in Dorset.

Not far off as the crow flies, but accessible by tortuous roads, Hilton should be seen for its church, which incorporates windows and fan vaulting from the cloisters of Milton Abbey. From the same source it acquired 12 early fifteenth-century painted panels, carefully restored a few years ago, representing the Apostles, all looking very much alive. Westward from Hilton the road curls with the hill, until suddenly, in a wide, lush valley to the south one sees what looks like a mirage or an optical illusion, a large house beside an even larger church. Descent and closer approach show them to be real enough. The house is now Milton Abbey School, and the church the Abbey Church.

The Abbey was founded for a community of secular clergy by Athelstan, probably about 838-41, but in 964 Edgar replaced them with Benedictines. At the Dissolution the Abbey buildings were bought by John Tregonwell, who gave the church to the townsmen of Milton Abbas, and lived himself in the Abbot's lodgings. In the eighteenth century the property and the manor were bought by one Joseph Damer, described by Walpole as 'the most arrogant and proud of men, with no foundation but great wealth and a match with the Duke of Dorset's daughter. His birth and parts were equally mean and contemptible.' It is to Damer that we must ascribe the present pattern of church, house, and village, not to mention landscape, but Walpole's assessment of him is not unjust, for however exquisite his taste, and in its way Milton Abbas approaches perfection, his inhumanity and ruthlessness deserve only censure.

At Damer's arrival the village of Milton Abbas stretched south from the church on both sides of the stream which Capability Brown dammed to form the existing lake. It had a market, a fair, a school, almshouses, and a brewery. It had 500 or 600 people. To Damer, who shortly became Lord Milton and later Earl of Dorchester, it was an eyesore and a nuisance, particularly the school, whose pupils clambered into his garden, stole his fruit, and frightened his game. He decided therefore to remove the entire village, to lay out the landscape in the best possible taste, and rebuild his own house. He would need some part of the population still, and them he would house half a mile off in a model village in full accord with the demands of eighteenth-century sensibility. He proceeded to carry out this plan with the utmost callousness.

By 1780 he had been able by reversion or purchase to obtain most of the properties he needed. One of the exceptions belonged to a solicitor whose refusal to sell Damer countered by deliberately flooding his house. The victim sued, and won. When a few days later the church bells rang, for it was Guy Fawkes' Day, Damer in his bitterness assumed that they were celebrating his defeat and to the anger of the villagers had them taken down. The trustees of the school had also fought to prevent him from moving it, but he won his case in this instance, and the school was transferred to Blandford.

The new village, meanwhile, had been built between 1773 and 1779 either by Sir William Chambers, who worked on Damer's house until his client's conduct became too much to endure, or by Brown. It has one street, the neatest possible, two rows of semi-detached cottages generously spaced, the new church in the middle of one row, and almshouses like those of Wimborne St. Giles, all running down a secluded and shallow vale. It has been interfered with only slightly and remains something of a work of art.

The Abbey church was never fully rebuilt after destruction by fire in 1309, and today only the choir and transepts survive. Splendid though the building is, conceived on a large and spacious scale, finely proportioned and elegant in detail, it has now a certain coldness, and though it should be seen it may possibly not be enjoyed. Sherborne Abbey and Wimborne Minster, the other comparable churches in Dorset, both seem to me to excel Milton in humanity and colour. There may be two reasons for this personal reaction. One is the irritating insistence of the authorities, when the church is open to the public, on relaying canned music of self-conscious solemnity and monotonous tempo. The other,

the ruthless stripping of the building by Damer's architect, James Wyatt. The transepts are utterly bare, to give emphasis to Carlini's admittedly fine monument to Lady Milton, and even the reredos of 1493, and the altar tomb of Sir John Tregonwell, do not compensate for a sense that much richness of detail has been lost.

The house was rebuilt in eighteenth-century gothic style by Chambers, who incorporated in it the great hall of the monastery with its fine hammer-beam roof. Most of the decoration in the house, which has some most delicately ornamented ceilings, was by Wyatt.

From the abbey grounds a green staircase of turf steps, understandably not open to the public, leads up to a little chapel overlooking church and house. It can be reached from the public road by a woodland path, and like other chapels on high places (at Abbotsbury, for instance) is dedicated to St. Catherine, because of the legend that she was buried on Mt. Sinai. Since she was also patron saint of spinsters this dark little cell, Transitional Norman in style, was frequented by young women seeking a husband with the prayer:

> *St. Catherine, St. Catherine*
> *O lend me thine aid*
> *And grant that I never may*
> *Die an old maid.*
> *A husband, St. Catherine,*
> *A good one, St. Catherine,*
> *But ar-a-one better than*
> *Nar-a-one, St. Catherine.*

(i.e. 'Any better than none, St. Catherine.')

A similar rhyme, varied slightly, was in use at Abbotsbury.

North of Milton a road leads fairly directly to Bulbarrow Hill, a viewpoint over Blackmore Vale regrettably well known, for on a sunny holiday, traffic becomes almost as complicated as by the sea at Weymouth. On the slope below, Ibberton sits snugly, its church overlooking it like an invigilator. 'Perpendicular' describes its architectural style, but its walls lean outward, and it has only two companions in England in its dedication to St. Eustace.

Beyond the ridge west of Milton runs the other Winterborne valley, giving its name to the villages along it. The stream rises at Winterborne Houghton, and flows to Winterborne Stickland, a potentially attractive village spoiled by infelicitous siting of a petrol station and utility sheds. Down the valley, which runs through gently sloping hills, often wooded, one reaches Winterborne Clenston, where the manor house, a satisfying work in the usual ashlar with bands of flint, has not changed hands by purchase in all the seven centuries during which its history can be traced. The house as it stands now was built at the end of the fifteenth century though some of it may be earlier. It has some pieces of Tudor plasterwork, an attic with cusped wind-braces (which suggests that the attic floor was a later addition, for such ornamentation is intended to be seen) and a room with an unusually early ribbed ceiling. The barn by the road has a hammer-beam roof with moulded timbers, which could hardly have been intended for this building, and may have come from Milton Abbey.

The church at Winterborne Whitchurch possesses yet another discard from Milton, this time its pulpit, which dates from the fifteenth century. It has also some thirteenth-century capitals carved with angel faces, and a curious font of 1450 paralleled at Bradford Abbas. John Wesley, son of Bartholomew Wesley of Charmouth, and grandfather of the founders of Methodism, was vicar here from 1658 until he was ejected in 1662. As an itinerant preacher thereafter he endured periods of imprisonment in Dorchester, Poole and Blandford, and died in 1670. A native of the village, George Turbervile, was secretary to Thomas Randolph, Elizabeth's ambassador to the court of Ivan the Terrible. He published verses on his Russian experiences, various other poems, and translations into English verse of Ovid and lesser Latin poets.

From here the stream wanders through progressively flatter country to Winterborne Kingston (where the Early English church, heavily restored, has a Jacobean pulpit and a late seventeenth-century font) and then with the road by its side to Anderson, where a Tregonwell manor house of 1622 in dark red brick with ashlar dressings stands withdrawn and solitary behind a formal garden. Apart from the church, nothing else remains of the village. Winterborne Tomson nearby, similarly evanescent, is merely a farm and a minute church—but what a church! A Norman apsidal building with a complete set of eighteenth-century oaken fittings—box pews, pulpit, and gallery, pale and crumbling under a fifteenth-century wagon roof, and all restored with the proceeds of a sale of Thomas Hardy manuscripts given for the purpose by the poet himself. The last Winterborne village, Zelston, small as it is, looks indecently solid after such fragility.

The Winterborne flows into the Stour near Wimborne Minster, and the Stour valley forms the next and the largest breach in the downs. The part of it covered in this chapter is conveniently bisected at Blandford Forum, a sensible point from which to explore eastern Dorset, since communications by road are good and Bournemouth, Poole, Wimborne, Shaftesbury, and Dorchester all reasonably accessible.

'Pleasant and hospitable' Blandford, as Gibbon called it, is an eighteenth-century town centred on its market place and its eighteenth-century church. Of its earlier existence only the most exiguous traces remain—the Ryves almshouse in Salisbury Street, and 'The Old House', east of the Post Office, built about 1660 by an eccentric German, Dr. Joachim Frederic Sagittary, who settled here and died in 1696. Almost everything else including the church and the school, where John Aubrey was once a pupil, disappeared in a fire in 1731. Like the fire at Dorchester in 1613, it began in a tallow-chandler's, and spread with irresistible speed. It destroyed three fire-engines in half an hour, and spared only 40 houses in the town. The neighbouring villages of Bryanston and Blandford St. Mary were almost totally razed.

At the eastern end of the market place a small Doric portico shelters a pump, and bears an inscription telling us that it was given by John Bastard in 1768 as a memorial of the fire in 1731 and a precaution against another. He also gave £600, of which the interest on £500 was to be used for 'teaching boys and girls to read and buy propor (*sic*) books', the interest on the balance to keep the pump in repair.

This John Bastard and his brother, William, were architects, and the sons of an architect, whom a memorial in the church describes as 'A man useful and industrious in his generation, a peaceable and inoffensive neighbour, and eminent for his skill in architecture'. He had married Bridget, the sister of Thomas Creech, who translated Lucretius, Horace, Theocritus, Manilius, and other Classical writers, and was himself a native of Blandford. John and William were in their forties when the fire cost their firm, Bastard & Co., £3,709/10/4 (they lost more than anyone else, it seems) and created for it a road to prosperity. Their portraits in the Town Hall show them both with alert eyes and confident faces, John plump, William thinner, and more hawklike, and the energy the artist has managed to suggest served Blandford, Dorset, and Bastard & Co. well. Much of Georgian Blandford was their work, including the town hall and the church, the old Greyhound Inn (now the National Provincial Bank building), the former Red Lion Inn, and other buildings. Their work was moreover not confined to Blandford. John Bastard built Sir Peter Thompson's house in Market Street, Poole, now used by the College of Art, and the work of Blandford architects can be found in several parts of the county—at Crichel, Moreton House, Whatcombe House, and Smedmore, for instance. Another Blandford architect, Francis Cartwright, of whom we do not know whether he competed or collaborated with the Bastards, built Came House, and worked at Stepleton and Creech Grange.

The Bastards' masterpiece is undoubtedly the parish church, a spacious and graceful building in green ashlar with box pews and a west gallery. The north and south galleries, added in the early nineteenth century, are shortly to be removed, to restore the original design of the architects. The carved and plush covered seat for the Mayor dates from 1748, and the organ is a particular gem, one of the few surviving works of George Pike England, said to have been made for the Savoy Chapel, in London, for which it proved too large, and to have been given to Blandford by George III. Although the town has a wealth of other good mid-eighteenth century buildings, as well as those already mentioned, the Old Bank House, north of the church, Coupar House and Lime Tree House, in Church Lane, and several groups in East Street, especially No. 5, are particularly fine.

Alfred Stevens, the sculptor, was born at Blandford in 1817, the son of a joiner, decorator, and heraldic painter with bad drinking habits and temper. He was rescued from his uninspiring home by Samuel Best, the Vicar of Blandford St. Mary, who, with other friends, sent him at the age of 15 to Italy. Nine years later he returned penniless to Blandford, having earned his living by his painting, worked with Thorwaldsen, and studied pre-Raphaelite art 12 years before the Movement of that name. It was at this time that he helped with the decorations at Chettle. In 1844 he left Dorset for good, but when he died in 1872 it was an old Blandford friend who acted as his executor.

At Bryanston the village has disappeared, and the old manor house was replaced in 1778 with a building by Wyatt, which gave way itself more than a century later to the present building, designed by Norman Shaw, and now a school. On the Blandford side of the river, south of the town is the site of another village where only house and church remain, Langton Long Blandford.

Both buildings are of the nineteenth century, but placed on a column in the nave of the church is a neat little fifteenth-century brass to John Whitewood and his two wives.

The main road to Wimborne and Poole follows the right bank of the Stour through Charlton Marshall, where the church (1713) was probably designed by Thomas Bastard, father of John and William, to Spettisbury, a long monotonous village overlooked by the small earthwork called Spettisbury Rings, or Crawford Castle, and partly redeemed by the variegated stone of its squat-towered church. A country road at the south end of the village leads over a nine-arched bridge of brown and grey stone towards Tarrant Crawford, once the site of an important abbey, of which the church and a long, low building with buttresses, part of a farm, are all that remain.

It was founded by Ralph de Kahaines (whose name is enshrined in that of the neighbouring village of Tarrant Keynston) in the twelfth century. His son William made over to it the tithe 'of all bread made in his house, and the salt pork, and the cattle killed in his house every year'. Yet the nuns of Tarrant later regarded as their founder Richard Poore, the Bishop of Salisbury, who began the building of Salisbury Cathedral, and was born and buried at Tarrant. He died in 1237, and when in the following year Joan, Queen of Scotland, daughter of King John, died on a visit to London she also was buried at Tarrant, 'according to her will'. The main feature of the church is an extraordinary set of fourteenth-century wall paintings, the length of the south wall of the nave being taken up with a life of St. Margaret of Antioch in 14 rust-coloured scenes, with, below, a Morality of the Three Living and the Three Dead. The main fabric of the building must date from Poore's time, but the roof is of the early fifteenth century, and the font with its cover, the altar rails, and pulpit, are Jacobean.

A country road leads up the valley of the Tarrant through or past all the villages that bear its name. At Tarrant Rushton, the third of them, which lies on high ground on the other side of the stream, the church is largely Norman, built in the form of a Greek cross of brown and grey stone and flint, very lively of texture. You must look hard for the church at Tarrant Rawston. This minute hamlet hides its little church, now disused, behind a farmyard and in the front garden of a house. On its ashlar and flint exterior the stone has weathered exquisitely, and the interior, though plain, has a Jacobean pulpit, early nineteenth-century pews, and a west gallery accessible from outside. Tarrant Monkton has a watersplash, and some thatched cottages. At Tarrant Hinton, just across the Blandford-Salisbury road, up a cul-de-sac richly furnished with cottages of cob and thatch, is a church of some character, partly Early English, partly Perpendicular, and possessed of a splendid Easter sepulchre of 1530.

The last of these villages, Tarrant Gunville, about which the hills of Cranborne Chase begin to close, sees the source of the Tarrant, which runs along the side of the road as a rivulet. The rectory, a Georgian house in bizarre stripes of flint and almost white ashlar, and the manor of the same period, flank the restored church, in the outside of which a memorial stone of 1567 has been incorporated, inscribed, 'All fowre be but one, earthe, fleshe, worme, and bone'.

Eastbury Park, immediately to the south, contains a remnant of what was once the grandest house in Dorset. The estate was purchased in the reign of Queen Anne by George Dodington, one of the Lords of Admiralty, who dying in 1720 without children, left it and his fortune to his nephew, George Bubb, son of a Weymouth apothecary. In 1717 he had commissioned Vanbrugh to design him a house at Eastbury, and Bubb, who took his uncle's name, inherited the uncompleted edifice too. It was not finished until 1738, having cost more than £140,000, an immense sum of money at the time. It ranked third in size of Vanbrugh's houses after Blenheim and Castle Howard. It was 570 feet wide, and comprised five courts, the central one before the main block, which had a huge portico and was flanked by wings to which it was connected by arcades.

The corpulent Bubb Dodington spent his life and quite a lot of his wealth in the corrupt politics of the day as a follower of Frederick, Prince of Wales, and a supporter of the Marquis of Bute. Weymouth and Melcombe Regis, which elected two members each to Parliament before the Reform Act, and were in fact the very rottenest of rotten boroughs, were totally in his pocket, and he ensured that they sent to the House many of his friends, relatives, and associates, one of the more interesting being Francis Dashwood, of the Hellfire Club and West Wycombe. In 1761, the year before his death, Dodington was created Lord Melcombe, a title which died with him. He was not merely a venal politician, but an assiduous host, and quite a character. Describing a visit to Eastbury, Richard Cumberland wrote of him that he 'had to the ladies all the courtly and profound devotion of a Spaniard, with the ease and gaiety of a Frenchman towards the men'. Although he possessed an abnormally extensive wardrobe, he refused to change the fashion of his clothes and to the end of his life continued wearing styles of the time of Anne and George I. Pictures he judged by their price, but possessed none, and decorated his walls with 'immense patches of gilt leather, shaped into bugle horns, upon hangings of rich crimson velvet'. His floors he covered with a carpet-substitute made from old clothes, in which pockets, buttonholes, and loops remained unconcealed. For all that, and despite a certain boorishness, he appears to have been something of a wit, and by Cumberland's testimony was 'an elegant Latin Classic', whose favourite author was Tacitus. Entertainment of his guests he achieved by reading aloud, though his choice of subject sometimes puzzled the eighteenth-century sense of propriety. During Cumberland's visit he read to a mixed company the whole of Fielding's *Jonathan Wild*, 'in which he certainly consulted his own turn for irony rather than theirs for elegance'

28 *Blandford Parish Church, from the west*

29   *Blandford Forum, the Town Hall*

30   *Blandford Forum*

He left Eastbury to his nephew, Lord Temple, who tried to get rid of it, even offering £200 *per annum* to anyone who would live in it, but found no takers and had most of it pulled down. The wing that remains looks squat and ordinary, rather like an undistinguished railway station, but for the arch leading into the courtyard, once the stable court. This arch, of monumental size, with enormous baroque volutes on either side, has two pine trees growing on top.

A road from Tarrant Rawston leads to Witchampton, a wooded village on a twisting hilly lane, with a seventeenth-century manor of great charm, and a restored church in which you may hear the Hallelujah Chorus for the pressing of a button, under the sardonic gaze of two heads, one grotesque, the other as agonised as a ravaged landscape.

At More Crichel, the splendid setting of the house was created like that of Milton by uprooting a village. The inhabitants were placed halfway to Witchampton, at Newton, where a paper mill still operates two centuries after its establishment. An earlier house had been burnt down in 1742 and the then occupier, Sir William Napier, began to rebuild, but in 1765 Crichel was inherited by Humphrey Sturt of Horton, whose father was responsible for the tower near that village. Sturt abandoned Horton for Crichel, and by addition and alteration built the house which stands today. James Wyatt and one of the Blandford architects were among those whose designs were used there.

North-west of Blandford the Stour valley opens out. The road to Sherborne crosses the river by an old bridge near Durweston, which it skirts, then runs along the foot of the hills on the right bank to Shillingstone, which may be regarded as a frontier village of Blackmore Vale. It has length with little breadth or interest, though its church has a twelfth-century core, and a fine Victorian wagon roof in the nave, painted, and furnished with elaborately carved gilded tie-beams. The village cross is fifteenth century, with a modern top.

The road to Shaftesbury, from which that to Sherborne parts at Durweston, twists and turns in a generally northerly direction between wooded hills in a narrow steep-sided valley through countryside but for the absence of vineyards less English than Rhenish. Down it flows the tiny river Iwerne, which meets the Stour at Stourpaine, a little village of some thatch and much brick. The most testing for the motorist of the many sharp bends in the road are those which carry it round the park at Stepleton House, which, with the church, is all that remains of the village of Iwerne Stepleton. The story goes that when the turnpike road to Shaftesbury was being planned, the commissioners who visited Stepleton to arrange for it to go through the park were lavishly entertained, and presented after a good dinner with a paper to sign containing 'a few trifling alterations'. They found too late that the route to which they had agreed was long and winding. Stepleton House was then owned by Peter Beckford, the author of *Thoughts on Hunting*. It seems to have been built at the end of the seventeenth century, and has eighteenth-century additions, which were probably incomplete when Beckford's father entertained Gibbon in 1762, for the historian found it 'unmeaning, expensive, and unfinished'. Its setting is spacious, its lawns, its chestnuts, beeches, limes, and planes, and its inevitable lake all carefully placed in the best eighteenth-century fashion.

Shroton, or Iwerne Courtney, a mile further north on the other side of the road has a decent church in seventeenth-century gothic. At the east end of the north aisle shut off by a contemporary carved timber screen is a memorial to Sir Thomas Freke, its broken pediment flanked by skulls with ears of corn projecting from the eye-sockets.

The village is dominated by Hambledon Hill, a spreadeagled island of chalk over 600 feet high, crowned with a garland of earthworks. The almost ploughed-out traces of a neolithic cause-wayed camp (about 2500 B.C.) precede on the east the triple ramparts of an Iron Age fortress frowning over the Stour valley and Blackmore Vale and enclosing a long barrow of about 1500 B.C. It was the scene in 1645 of a curious encounter. In that year in several western and west midland counties country folk, sick and tired of pillage by both sides in the Civil War, banded together to defend their own interests, calling themselves Clubmen. In Dorset they began by attacking the Royalists, and Col. Bingham sent them help from Poole. They seem then to have come under the leadership of some of the local Royalists, and to have turned their attention to the Parliamentary forces, whom they harried at Sturminster Newton, as well as in south Dorset. A great gathering at Badbury Rings resulted in a petition to both Fairfax and King Charles to stop the war, but of course both sides, while proclaiming their willingness to do so, regretted that the belligerency of their opponents prevented them. A scuffle on Castle Hill, Shaftesbury, finished with the capture of 50 ring-leaders by one of Fairfax's officers, and in August 2000 Clubmen under several clergymen, notably Thomas Bravell, rector of Compton Abbas (near Shaftesbury), and convenor of the force, gathered on Hambledon Hill. No less than Cromwell himself came to the foot of the hill and advised them to disperse. On their refusal he sent up a lieutenant with 50 men, who were fired upon, despite Cromwell's avowal of his peaceful intentions. A third time he gave them a chance to avoid bloodshed, but Bravell cried that 'they must stand to it now', and that he 'would pistol them that gave back'. The Parliamentarians then stormed the ramparts with little loss, and scattered the Clubmen, some of whom escaped by sliding ignominiously down the ramparts, though 300 were taken prisoner and herded into Shroton church. Cromwell wrote to Fairfax, 'I believe I killed not twelve of them, but cut very many and put them all to flight.' Many of them, he went on, were 'poor, silly creatures whom if you please to let me send home they promise to be very dutiful for some time to come and will be hanged before they come out again'. More than a century later Wolfe encamped his men at Shroton Lines, on the north side of Hambledon, before embarking for the voyage to Quebec.

The road from Stepleton to Child Okeford divides Hambledon from Hod Hill, lower than Hambledon, and bearing a smaller Iron Age encampment, its interior still pock-marked with traces of storage pits. In the north-west corner Vespasian's soldiers placed a camp of their own, about A.D. 43-5 occupying it for some 20 years as the headquarters of a garrison which held the surrounding country in subjection, and its traces can be clearly seen.

CHAPTER SIX

The North — Shaftesbury, Sherborne, and Blackmore Vale

Other towns in Dorset lie in valleys, or combes and coves, over-looked by hills or cliffs, or spread placidly like Poole and Wim-borne into flat lands by the side of rivers or over a gently undulat-ing heath. Shaftesbury, or Shaston, as it used to be called, crowns a hill-top, a spur of greensand commanding superb views over the eastern part of Blackmore Vale. From all directions one ap-proaches it uphill, sometimes through spectacular countryside. The road from Sixpenny Handley across the greenest and woodiest part of Cranborne Chase, dips into Tollard Royal, which hides in a tree-shaded vale, technically in Wiltshire. It then climbs fairly sharply to within a few hundred yards of the Dorset bor-der, which it still keeps between itself and Ashmore, where a cluster of houses more or less surround a circular pond of great antiquity and durability even in drought. Passing close to Win Green Hill, the highest point in Wiltshire, it runs along the edge of Charlton Down, to cross the county border and drop suddenly through a series of violent turns on the wooded stretch known as the Zigzag before rising again less urgently into Shaftes-bury itself. From Blandford two routes may be taken. One leads over the hills, fairly straight (it was a turnpike), east of the main road and unimpaired by villages. After the viewpoint on Spread-eagle Hill it falls, winding, steep and narrow into Melbury Abbas, then up again into Shaftesbury. The other road from Blandford, the main route, we followed in the last chapter to the defile by Hambledon Hill and Shroton. Thence it continues waywardly beneath the grassy rampart that forms the eastern rim of Black-more Vale, each turn showing green and sometimes startling vistas of great variety, until it climbs to Shaftesbury by a long and steep slope. From the north and west the approaches are less interesting, though the countryside of the Vale must surely please anyone who enjoys green fields, hedgerows, and a profusion of oaks and beeches.

Having reached the town, the visitor who knows of its association with Alfred the Great and Canute, and has come across mention of its Abbey, and its sometime wealth of churches, will suffer acute disappointment if he expects to find a lesser York or Winchester. Of course, everyone must enjoy its superb situation, especially the view from Park Hill over eastern Black-more to Bulbarrow in the usually hazy distance, and the romantic sight of the countryside beyond the steep and cobbled lane, Gold Hill, down which the town cascades under the stoutly buttressed wall, green with moss and lichen, that once bounded the Abbey. Yet apart from this episode of scenic drama, Shaftesbury is one of Dorset's plainer towns, its antiquities with few exceptions obliterated, its past obscured.

Geoffrey of Monmouth says it was Caer Palladur to the Ancient Britons, built by Lud, or Ludhudibras, son of Leil, eighth king of the Britons from Brutus. Unfortunately for the lovable Geoffrey's gossip, although it may have been a British settlement before the Romans arrived, there is no evidence that it was, or even that the Romans themselves occupied the site. We know nothing until the foundation of the Abbey in 888 as a Benedictine nunnery, traditionally ascribed to Alfred the Great, whose daughter, Aethelgiva was the first Abbess. Yet even that date is uncertain. That the Abbey existed and flourished by 978 the story of Edward the Martyr's second burial here attests, and St. Elgiva, the queen of Edmund I, was buried here in the mid-tenth century. The shrine of Edward the Martyr brought the Abbey fame and wealth. Pilgrims flocked to it, it acquired land and influence, the Abbess ranked as a Baroness, and men said that if the Abbess of Shaston married the Abbot of Glaston their heir would own more land than the king. In 1035 Canute died here, though he was buried at Winchester. In 1313 the Abbey for a few months was a prison for the wife of Robert Bruce who had been betrayed to the English in her husband's absence by the Earl of Ross in 1306. In 1507 the Abbess was providing hospitality for Catharine of Aragon on her way from Plymouth to London to marry Arthur, Henry VII's eldest son. Of all the Abbesses, who before 1066 were appointed by the King, and afterwards were elected by the nuns subject always to the King's approval, the most interesting was the learned Marie de France. She was daughter of Geoffrey of Anjou, and half-sister to Henry II, and a poetess, who not only wrote ballads of her own, but translated Aesop and the *Purgatory of St. Patrick* into French from English.

As usual, the town flourished with the Abbey. Athelstan licensed two mints here, Edward the Confessor a third, and in due course Shaftesbury acquired fairs and markets—when sheep were penned between the buttresses of Gold Hill, and a fish market was held below St. Peter's Church. It had difficulty perennially, however, with water, for the wells which supplied its needs were at the bottom of the hill in the parish of St. James to the south or at Enmore Green to the north. In early days water was brought up by man or pack horse, and even a reservoir near the top of Gold Hill was supplied manually in this way. Each year on Holy Cross Day, later the Monday before Ascension Day, the Mayor and Burgesses walked in procession to Enmore Green carrying a byzant (or besom) decorated 'like a May-garland, with gold and peacock's feathers' and accompanied by the most recently married couple in the borough, called Lord and Lady for the occasion. They handed over a raw calf's head, a pair of gloves, a gallon of beer, and two penny loaves to the steward of the Manor of Gillingham, where Enmore Green belonged, as a payment for the town's water. When once the Mayor refused to countenance the ceremony, the people of Enmore Green closed the wells to their neighbours on the hill, but the custom was discontinued on grounds of expense in 1830. From the middle of the last century water has been pumped to the town mechanically, and the last byzant is now in the Town Hall.

The foundations of the Abbey were uncovered in 1861, and can be seen—heaps of stones where the piers were, lines of stones, several feet wide, showing the footings of the walls. There are several stone coffins and graves, a stone cross with alabaster inlays, and in a little modern shelter a few bones found nearby in a lead casket in 1931 and identified with reasonable probability as those of Edward the Martyr. The small museum in the Abbey grounds contains a large number of stone fragments, some of them extraordinarily delicately carved, and some, such as the head of a mailed knight in creamy Purbeck marble, firm and powerful.

Of Shaftesbury's 12 medieval churches only St. Peter's remains, and that in poor condition, though now undergoing restoration. Eight of the rest have disappeared, and the other three the Victorians pulled down and completely re-built. Otherwise nothing remains to remind anyone of Shaftesbury's history but a handful of eighteenth-century houses and a Georgian hotel in the Market Place.

Below Shaftesbury and north of the chalk downs the scenery becomes less dramatic than in the centre and west of the county, or along the coastal strip. The basin of the upper Stour—and that essentially is what is meant by Blackmore Vale—is a region of clay broken by strips of limestone. The result after some centuries of deforestation is a landscape of small fields and hedgerows punctuated lavishly by trees sometimes grouped into coppices, crossed by roads that wind, rise and fall enough to give variety to the scenery without in any way suggesting ruggedness or wildness. The country roads often have broad verges, if narrow carriageways, the numerous villages sprawl shapelessly. All in all, Blackmore has the kind of countryside often thought of as typically English, with some individual features of its own.

South of Shaftesbury is a line of villages near the Blandford road under the edge of the Cranborne Chase hills. Of these, Iwerne Minster, a largely modern village in red brick, has an attractive church with one of Dorset's three medieval spires, a north arcade of massive Norman work (immense piers and scallop capitals) and a Transitional south arcade. When the Victorians built a new chancel they moved the Norman chancel arch to the south aisle, which is also Norman and may conceivably stand on the site of a Saxon nave. The pulpit, now without a tester, is Jacobean.

Compton Abbas stands rather higher up the hills than the other neighbouring villages, and its decent church of 1868 is situated with a good view to south and west. The building it superseded, the church of the soldierly and royalist Mr. Bravell who fought Cromwell on Hambledon Hill, was more than half a mile away. Its fifteenth century tower remains, a ruin in its old churchyard with one or two dilapidated table tombs and gravestones like faithful old retainers to an impoverished elderly nobleman. The setting, an enormous natural amphitheatre composed of Melbury Hill and Compton and Fontmell Downs, is lordly enough to give the simile point.

Four miles north-east of Shaftesbury, reached by a road through sparsely populated, flat country, Gillingham is the first considerable settlement in the course of the Stour, which rises another four miles to the north at Stourhead, near Zeals, in Wiltshire. Gillingham today is an agglomeration of modern buildings without merit. Even its few eighteenth-century buildings seem affected by the prevalent mediocrity, though it was once a Royal Manor and the centre of a Forest. Close by Edmund Ironside defeated Canute in 1016, in the battle which secured him control of southern England. Here, 36 years later, a Witanagemot approved the succession of Edward the Confessor in preference to Edmund's children whom Canute had exiled to Hungary. Just east of the town the earthwork known as King's Court represents all that remains of a Plantagenet hunting lodge, which Henry I visited in 1132 and John (of course!) three times. Henry III had much repair work done, but after his successor's reign the place was allowed to decay, and in the eighteenth century the remaining stones were used for repairing the road to Shaftesbury. The rather gloomy church has some fifteenth-century bench-ends with grotesque poppyheads, and two good, large monuments, one to the brothers Jessup who were respectively vicar and physician, and whose Jacobean effigies lie side by side, the other to Francis Dirdoe, who died in 1733, and whose full-length, full-size portrait in flowing drapery like a Roman matron accompanies those of the two sisters she left as executrices. The small museum has some good local material.

Gillingham is the centre of a Dorset salient thrust into Somerset and Wiltshire, its base formed by the A 30, which cuts it off from the rest of Dorset. Apart from Gillingham, though the countryside is pleasant enough in a quiet way, there is little to see. The villages—Motcombe, Bourton, Kington Magna, Milton-on-Stour—are not only visually dull, but have little history. But Silton, on a narrow side road south of Zeals, has a splendid church on a knoll overlooking an insignificant village. The roofs of the nave, south aisle, and porch, are all excellent, there is a north chapel with fan-vaulting and a large baroque monument by John Nost to a seventeenth-century judge, Sir Hugh Wyndham, who postures in stone life-size, in judicial stance, accompanied by two mourning female figures. At Buckhorn Weston, reached from Gillingham by tortuous roads spanning the land like a web the little brown and grey-green church has a porch 20° out of the vertical, leaning drunkenly against the nave, and six painted panels said to be by Thornhill. On the north side of the chancel a tomb bears an effigy of a man in the civilian dress of the fourteenth century, supposedly one Alexander Mowbray, who died in 1410, though the tomb has no inscription.

West Stour, just off the A 30, has a few eighteenth-century houses in grey-gold stone, while further east, on the main road, at East Stour the church is a startling piece of Victorian Norman, with a massive, squat, battlemented central tower, and a crossing beneath it proportionately impressive. West of the church an early nineteenth-century house in grey-gold stone with dressings of green ashlar stands on the site of the old Manor House which Henry Fielding inherited and occupied for three years, during which he ran through his fortune. The consequent penury turned him into a professional author, and he was able to draw on at least some of his Dorset experiences, for the Rector of West Stour, William Young, was the original of Parson Adams, and Parson Trulliber is supposed to have been modelled on a curate of Motcombe named Oliver. Fielding later collaborated with Young in translating the *Plutus* of Aristophanes.

South of the main road, Stour Provost stands on high ground over the Stour valley, just off the road from Gillingham to Sturminster Newton. Its centre is a cross roads of which the northern and western arms are culs-de-sac, its houses are mainly of yellow stone, many of them thatched, and all old, and the village has shape and character, which most of the Vale settlements on lower ground lack. The church, though heavily restored, has a fifteenth-century panelled roof in the chancel, and a window with good modern glass in the north wall of the nave. Across the river is Fifehead Magdalen, a prosperous looking place in the pale yellow local stone. The church contains a very large monument with no fewer than six life-sized portrait busts, all lively, of Sir Richard Newman, his wife Lady Frances, their son, Sir Samuel, and their three daughters. They all died from 1721 onwards, and the monument also commemorates three other children who died 'young'.

Nearer Sturminster Newton, Marnhull (Marlott, the home of

Hardy's Tess) is a large scattered, mixed village, hilly and rambling. Its church is its particular feature—the best, perhaps, in the whole Vale. It has a handsome fifteenth-century tower with pinnacled buttresses, and the fifteenth-century nave roof consists of carved panels, each one different. A contemporary tomb with three effigies, a fourteenth-century roof of the trussed rafter type in the north aisle, fragments of Tudor wall paintings and a profusion of hatchments all attest the building's antiquity.

Further south, on the same ridge of Corallian limestone, is Hinton St. Mary, which is unprepossessing from the main road, but attractive enough off it, especially round the church. The carefully groomed manor house dates from the seventeenth century, and was the home of William Freke, who wrote in 1693 *A Dialogue by way of Question and Answer concerning the Deity; to which is added a clear and brief Confutation of the Doctrine of the Trinity*. Members of Parliament, to several of whom he sent copies, had them burned publicly, while their author was fined £500 for blasphemy and ordered to make a recantation in court. He also published two books on dreams. 'A medley of folly, obscenity, and blasphemy', comments Hutchins, adding, 'His understanding was deranged, but he acted as a justice of the peace many years.' In 1963 a large Roman mosaic was found in the village, dating from the second half of the fourth century and bearing not only the Christian Chi-Rho symbol, but a human bust probably representing Christ. If this supposition is right it is the earliest example in Britain. The mosaic is now in the British Museum.

A mile or so further on, in a great bend of the Stour as it breaks through the low ridge, Sturminster Newton watches the passing traffic from Blandford to Sherborne and Shepton Mallet from a safe distance, protected by the river and a handsome bridge of six arches. It has the feel of a country town that really moves at a slower pace than the rest of the modern world, some of its houses dating from the eighteenth century, roofed with thatch or tiles, its shops occasionally bow-fronted, its streets narrow. One of its inns, the White Hart, has particularly attractive thatch and dormer windows. The church, which was almost entirely rebuilt in 1827, has a good fifteenth-century waggon roof with finely carved bosses, and angels at wall-plate level, while the lectern is a memorial to Barnes, who was born in the parish. Hardy lived in Sturminster while writing *The Return of the Native* from 1876 to 1878, though the primeval landscape of the novel could hardly differ more from the domesticated dairy lands in this district. Across the river, Newton, along the main road, has a pretty group of Georgian houses, plastered, thatched, and colourful, which the traffic has no time to stop and admire, while on Castle Hill immediately above it is the ruin not of a castle, but of a stone house, perhaps medieval. Below the main road and on the river bank an old mill with some seventeenth-century brickwork and a roof partly tiled in stone, has an impressive weir and a view worthy of Constable.

A mile or so downstream, at Fiddleford, is another, older mill. The little building by what was apparently the mill-race has an inscription dated 1556, and a barely decipherable text which reads:

> *He that wyll have anythinge done.*
> *Let him com fryndly he shall be welcom:*
> *A frynd to the owner and enemy to no man*
> *Pass all here freely to com when they can,*
> *For the tale of troth I do always professe;*
> *Myller be true, disgrace not thy vest.*
> *If falsehood appeare the fault shall be thyne,*
> *And of sharpe punishment think me not unkind.*

In the long grey house nearby with stone tiled-roof and stone-mullioned windows, one can see from the gate a Tudor door and an early Tudor three-light window. Further upstream still, reached easily from the road to Shaftesbury, Hammoon may be visited for its remoteness and the dignified charm of its thatched grey stone manor house. In the tiny church is an Early English chancel, a fifteenth-century panelled roof, and a pulpit of 1635, with contemporary altar rails. The choir stalls probably early sixteenth century, were imported from East Anglia, and the early fifteenth-century wooden reredos from a builder's yard near London, both in 1946.

In the southern part of the Vale, one approaches Fifehead Neville from Sturminster by a ford across the river Divelish, or on foot over a pack-horse bridge in golden stone with two pointed arches and a cutwater. In the church, a large monument to Robert Ryves, who died in 1658, describes him as 'a sincere lover of the royail family, for which he suffered much in the time of rebellious persecution'.

Another victim of the Civil War was Thomas Clarke, rector of Hazelbury Bryan, whose son was shot dead in a skirmish with Roundhead soldiers on the road to Weymouth, and who was ejected from his living in 1645. At the Restoration the 'intruder' was in turn expelled because he had said in a sermon that 'the queen-mother was a whore and all her children bastards, and publicly prayed for the destruction of the Royal family root and branch'. His fifteenth-century church, perhaps the handsomest in the Vale after Marnhull, has an exquisite tower of varied stone, grey, gold, and brown, first-rate roofs, an eighteenth-century pulpit, and some fragments of old glass.

At Mappowder also the church is a great delight, with a pinnacled tower and gargoyles of distinction. Its Perpendicular interior is superbly light, and there are some good monuments to the Coker family, who, originating at Coker in Somerset, came to the manor of Mappowder by marriage in the reign of Henry V. The church has a little stone effigy of a knight in thirteenth-century armour holding what appears to be a heart. What this means is open to conjecture, but the most likely guess is that his heart alone was brought back from Crusading for burial here.

At Buckland Newton, on the edge of Vale and Downs, brownish stucco rendering outside and an unfortunately chosen colour wash within spoil the church in a village which could do with lifting out of the ordinary, but the chancel is good Early English, and some details and fittings are worth noticing. At Pulham the eighteenth-century gothic Old Rectory and the church are isolated, and the latter is worth visiting for some finely carved corbels of the thirteenth century.

Kingstag, not far off, is nondescript, but allegedly named from a romantic story. In early Plantagenet times Blackmore was a Royal Forest. While hunting in the neighbourhood on one occasion, Henry III saw a white hart, which he ordered to be spared, but one of his party, Thomas de la Lynde, killed the creature nevertheless. In fury, Henry fined de la Lynde and his companions, and laid on them in perpetuity a tax known as White Hart Silver. The evidence for the tax is disputable, and its exact nature obscure. Thomas Fuller says he actually paid it, remarking: 'Myself hath paid a share for the sauce who never tasted any of the meat; so that it seems King's Venison is sooner eaten than digested'. The name Kingstag is supposed to commemorate de la Lynde's misdemeanour, and for centuries Blackmore was alternatively called the Vale of the White Hart.

Kingstag did have an authentic worthy of its own in the nineteenth century, a man called John Buckland, known round about as 'Doctor' Buckland. At the change of the moon in May he would hold what he called a 'twoad vair' for the cure of scrofula and running or tuberculous wounds. He would make a collection of toads, his patient would bare his chest, and Buckland, having seized and decapitated a toad would suspend it in a muslin bag round the sufferer's neck. If the unfortunate invalid became faint at the 'scrablen' of the creature's legs in its death throes he would die, otherwise he would be cured.

North of Kingstag on the main road from Blandford to Sherborne, one may usually see the herd of deer in the park at Stock Gaylard, where Stock House, a Georgian building approached by a long drive from the road, stands next to the church. Turning left at Lydlinch Common one reaches Stalbridge three miles further on, having passed on the way Thornhill, the ancestral home of the artist, which had left the family in an earlier generation, and which he re-purchased and rebuilt. Although Stalbridge has some houses of the seventeenth and eighteenth centuries, and a market cross in fair condition, it is a dull town on the whole. In the drastically restored church, on high ground opposite a group of early nineteenth-century houses, the north chapel has two fifteenth-century table tombs, one with a cadaverous effigy in a shroud. Stalbridge Park once contained the home of Robert Boyle, the chemist, the seventh son and fourteenth child of the Earl of Cork, who brought him here and placed him in the tutelage of the Rector. In 1643 he inherited the manor, where he worked from 1646 for about four years.

Westward the country is strongly under the influence of Sherborne, which forms a minor centre of trade and communications (nowadays overshadowed by Yeovil), but for many centuries was the natural capital of this part of England. It is a mellow town in the warm, butter-coloured stone quarried not far off at Ham Hill, in Somerset. Lying in a vale on the upper reaches of the Yeo, it looks comfortable and placid, dominated and unified by the square tower of the Abbey church, when seen in the filmy light of a summer afternoon sun from, say, Dancing Hill on the Dorchester road. A romantic description, perhaps, in which the outlines are blurred, the visually squalid subtopian outskirts forgotten, the best viewpoint and the finest weather deliberately chosen to exclude the outlook from the railway station in the rain. But Sherborne is one of these rare places where the weather seems to matter very little, and the town's friendliness metaphorical and literal overlies any unfortunate memory of grey skies reflected from puddles and wet-glossy pavements. Never dead-and-alive, going about its business at its own pace, despite its position on a trunk road, it lacks the no-nonsense commercialism of Dorchester. Of course, it also lacks Dorchester's

31 *Sturminster Newton: medieval six-arched bridge on the River Stour*

responsibilities, not being the county town.

Its history begins in 705, when King Ine of Wessex founded a bishopric here (though it is reasonable to suppose that there was already an ecclesiastical establishment in Sherborne). The diocese was extensive, including most of the south-west, until in 909 other dioceses were established at Wells, Crediton, and Ramsbury, after which the Bishop of Sherborne's jurisdiction extended only to Dorset. Aldhelm, the first Bishop, was a great scholar, the first Anglo-Saxon known to have written in Latin, and was later canonised. At least three of the early bishops fell in action against the Danes, one of them, Althstan, becoming King Ethulwulf's general-in-chief. The two older brothers of Alfred the Great, Ethelbald and Ethelbert, who died respectively in 860 and 866 are said to have been buried in the church, and Sherborne can be regarded, indeed, as the capital of Wessex at this time. The tradition that Alfred was educated here is unsupported (though not inherently absurd) but there is evidence that he was in Sherborne in 865 in person—and surely there were other occasions, too. Asser, a Welshman, and author of a biography of King Alfred, died in 909 and was the last Bishop of the diocese in its earlier form.

In 998 during the reign of Ethelred a Benedictine foundation in preparation for the Second Coming, scheduled for two years later, replaced the establishment of secular canons which dated from 705 or earlier. Less than a century afterwards, in 1075, Bishop Hermann moved the see to Salisbury, and left Sherborne with only the abbey, the Bishop remaining Abbot *ex officio* until 1122, when the offices were separated. In 1107 Bishop Roger pulled down the Saxon abbey church and rebuilt it, the core of the present building representing his work.

During the Middle Ages a flourishing community grew up round the Abbey, not merely to serve the needs of the monks, but independently through the manufacture of cloth and woollen goods. By the end of the fourteenth century a separate parish church, Allhalowes, had been built at the west end of the Abbey church, though it was pulled down at the Dissolution, and a general restoration undertaken in the following century. At this time a squabble with serious consequences developed between the townsmen and the monks. The parish church being insufficient for its functions, baptisms took place in the font of the Abbey church, which the abbot for some reason moved to an inconvenient place, whereupon the townsmen set up their own font in the parish church, and to the annoyance of the monks rang their own bells. In 1437 the Bishop ordered the restoration of the old font to its earlier position, the widening of the access to it, and the removal of the townsmen's font. Still, neither side was happy, and the font in Allhalowes remained. When the monks arranged for a butcher to deface it, the townsmen rioted. A parish priest shot a flaming arrow into the partition between the parts of the Abbey church used by the monks and the parish, and the church was set ablaze. The stonework reddened by the fire on the pillars west of the tower can still be seen. Since restoration was already in progress it went forward with the repair of this damage, and at the Dissolution when Sir John Horsey, the recipient of the abbey site and many of its possessions, sold the church to the townsfolk for £320, he delivered a complete edifice.

Despite some alterations it remains in essence much as it was, a building of rich detail and real grandeur. Basically it is a church of the twelfth century, the transepts and the north and south nave walls dating from Bishop Roger's day, and the fifteenth-century panelling on the piers of the nave arcades concealing an older core. The north and south arcades are not quite in line, the northern piers standing very slightly west of the southern, and the arches vary in width. It has been suggested that the piers were in fact those of the Saxon church which for reasons now unknown were not demolished when the crossing was rebuilt. However that may be the bays of the fifteenth-century clerestory were set out regularly and therefore do not correspond with the arches in the arcades of the nave. The west wall is largely Saxon, and a doorway at the west end of the north aisle dates from the late tenth century. The presbytery and ambulatory are fifteenth century, like the superb fan-vaulting of the nave and choir. The Lady Chapel, the eastern end of which is modern, and furnished with a handsome reredos of black and white engraved glass by Lawrence Whistler, is entered by an exquisite Early English arch. Since this is not quite in line with the choir, the fifteenth-century architects faced an awkward problem in designing the vaulting, and solved it by suspending a corbel like a stalactite from the roof near the southern respond of the arch.

Fragments of three Abbots' tombs are preserved in the aisles of the presbytery, the oldest a fragment of dark green Purbeck marble with the carved face of Abbot Clement, who died in 1160. On the west wall of the south transept is a huge monument by John Nost to John Digby, third Earl of Bristol, a flamboyant, grandiose affair like an oratorio, the Earl and his two wives posed theatrically on pedestals under an arched cornice with Corinthian side-columns by each of which weeps a *putto*. On the other side of the wall, in St. Katherine's Chapel, an altar tomb with effigies and canopy commemorates John Leweston and his wife, who died late in Elizabeth's reign. In the Wykeham chapel another altar tomb, similarly elaborate, but 20 years earlier, bears the recumbent likenesses in grey stone (it contrasts beautifully with the predominant gold) of Sir John Horsey and his son and namesake, both looking humourlessly mulish. Fragmentary medieval glass remains in the windows of the Chapel of St. Mary-le-Bow and more plentifully in St. Katherine's Chapel. The choir stalls, largely modern, have some fifteenth-century carved elbow rests and misericords.

Across the green, south-west of the church, the fifteenth-century almshouses, still in use for their original purpose, are built on the pattern of a monastic infirmary, where the chancel becomes the chapel and the nave the hall. The chapel has an original oak screen and a south window filled (very rare in Dorset) with original glass. It should on no account be missed not only for these features, but for the triptych behind the altar, painted late in the fifteenth century by an unknown artist, probably German, of great ability. Its three panels, depicting Christ performing miracles, have enormous vitality and the life-enhancing quality that for Berenson was the criterion of great art. The saints on the backs of the wings, judged by the same standards, are worthy of the rest.

Sherborne School adjoins the church, and in fact contains some of the Abbey buildings, namely the west range of the cloister, which perhaps originally incorporated the Abbey guest hall, and a block to the north, once the hall of the Abbot's lodging. The School dates back possibly to the founding of the Abbey in 705, and in the eleventh century St. Stephen Harding, founder of the Cistercian Order, was educated here. In 1540 the school building passed with the rest of the Abbey to Horsey, who left its educational activities undisturbed. In 1550 it received a Charter, virtually a second founding, from Edward VI, and later Horsey leased the Schoolhouse formally to the Governors. In 1605 the lease was extended to a thousand years.

A fifteenth-century gateway at the eastern end of the churchyard leads to a narrow passageway to the Conduit, a hexagonal structure of stone, which originally stood in the cloister and was used as the monk's washhouse. On the other side of the churchyard a range of shops in Half Moon Street dates from the early sixteenth century, and so does the building called Becket's Chapel, at the top of Cheap Street, while the adjoining inn and shops, though mainly later, have some fragments of the same date. All through the town centre one comes across relics of the Tudor, Stuart, and Hanoverian periods, some of them highly attractive. The timber framed Conservative Club, for instance, is partly seventeenth century, and Abbeylands, in Cheap Street, is rather

earlier, with an addition of 1649. Lord Digby's School, in New-
land, is a splendid and dignified house, its main block built about
1720 by one of the Bastards of Blandford, and containing paintings by Thornhill. In the same street stands the Manor House,
now used as the office of Sherborne U.D.C., incorporating some
work of about 1500. In Long Street, the Red House is conspicuous
by its colour, being built at the end of the seventeenth century
and refaced in red brick about 1730. The Eastbury Hotel, Abbots
Litton, and Bank House all give this street a touch of distinction.
In fact, Sherborne can show more numerous and varied examples
in architectural history, and in a less spoiled setting, than any
town in Dorset.

East of the town are the ruins of the old castle of Sherborne,
apart from Corfe the only extensive remains of a medieval castle
in the county. It was built originally by Bishop Roger of Sarum,
who undertook the first rebuilding of the Abbey church. The
manor had been acquired by the bishopric of Salisbury through St
Osmund of Seez, who, having come over with the Conqueror as a
knight and served him well, was rewarded with, among other
prizes, the Earldom of Dorset and the barony of Sherborne. In
old age he repented the blood he had shed, and took to the religious life, despite the reluctance of his King, who made him
Bishop of Salisbury to keep him in the nobility. Thereupon he
gave Sherborne to the bishopric, attaching to it this curse—'that
whosoever should take these lands from the bishopric or diminish
them in great or in small, should be accursed not only in this
world but also in the world to come unless in his lifetime he
made restitution thereof.' Naturally, people recalled the curse
in later years whenever a secular tenant or owner came to a bad
end, which in the Middle Ages was an occupational hazard among
owners and tenants of castles, even unaccursed.

Late in the reign of Elizabeth, the Bishops of Salisbury again
held Sherborne Castle, though local landowners such as the
Horseys and the Fitzjameses envied them fairly actively. It so

happened on one occasion that the Queen's favourite, Sir Walter Raleigh, riding between Plymouth and London, caught sight of Sherborne and, enchanted, set his heart upon it, undeterred by an ominous fall from his horse even as he gazed. He pestered the Queen for it, even giving her a jewel worth £250 'to make the Bishop'. Whether because he shared the current popular dislike of Raleigh, or because he remembered Osmund's curse or for some other reason, its Lord shrank from letting it go, but she persuaded him in 1592 to demise it to her, whereupon she transferred the lease to Sir Walter for a rent of £260, to be paid to the Bishop. According to Hutchins, the wretched man was 'surprised' into consenting, and never enjoyed himself afterwards.

At first Raleigh started to alter the medieval castle, but soon decided to build afresh on a nearby site, the house he raised forming the centre block of the mansion now called Sherborne Castle. On his fall from favour with Elizabeth, which happened very shortly after he obtained Sherborne, he was allowed to keep it, but after he had been found guilty of treason in 1603 and imprisoned in the Tower, the estate again aroused an unassuageable envy, this time in James I's unsavoury creature, Robert Carr. Owing to a technical legal fault in a document by which Sir Walter conveyed the estate to his son, Wat, James dispossessed Raleigh despite his anguish and his wife's violent protests, to which the King's only reply was 'I mun have the land, I mun have it for Carr'. The anger of the heir to the throne, Raleigh's friend, Prince Henry, persuaded James to make Carr disgorge it for £2,500 to the prince, whose intention to return it to Raleigh was frustrated by his unexpected death, men said by poison, whereupon James gave it back to his favourite. When later Carr was executed, James gave it to Sir John Digby, Earl of Bristol, in the face of a petition by Carew Raleigh, Sir Walter's only surviving son, who continued through his life to try for the return of the property he should have inherited. It seems that his first attempts after his father's execution in 1618 failed literally because James did not like his face, which reminded him of Sir

Walter. After James' death, King Charles I told Carew Raleigh that as prince he had promised for £10,000 to secure the title to Sherborne for the Earl of Bristol against Sir Walter's heirs, and could therefore not help. As late as 1651, when Digby had fled to France, Raleigh petitioned Parliament for the return of his inheritance, but had to be contented with an award of £500 per year out of the Digby estate.

The Civil War meanwhile had seen the end of the old castle. In 1642 the Marquis of Hertford had garrisoned and fortified it for the King against the Earl of Bedford, who laid siege to it in September. Bedford's sister, who was married to George, Lord Digby, son of the Earl of Bristol, was in the castle at the time, and Bedford sent her a message telling her to leave it since Parliament had ordered him to demolish it. Far from obeying, she rode to his camp and told him that if he carried out his orders 'he should find his sister's bones in the ruins'. Whether or not he was influenced by her he failed to press his attack, and for three years Sherborne stayed with the King. In July 1645, however, Fairfax invested the castle closely despite the diversion caused by the Clubmen, and in mid-August took it. On the instructions of Parliament it was 'slighted'. Only part of the curtain wall and the ruins of the keep and domestic buildings remain.

Raleigh's house, on the site of an older building just south of the old castle, was rectangular with hexagonal turrets at the corners. To it Lord Digby added four wings, so that the plan became a letter H, of which Raleigh's contribution was the cross piece. Since Digby added a hexagonal tower at the extremity of each wing, the place fairly bristles with hexagons, all forested with chimneys and finials. The whole building wears a covering of brownish stucco that looks peculiarly unprepossessing when wet. Some features associated with Raleigh remain, though much alteration has obliterated most of his work. The entrance hall and the small room north of it are distinctly of the late sixteenth century. The oak room, with its seventeenth-century brown stained oak panelling and the oak enclosures for its doorways, is delicious, and so in its more feminine way is the library, done in Strawberry Hill gothic in the late eighteenth century. The room (now a bathroom) adjoining Lady Bristol's room has an elaborate brass lock with a figure of a man (whose boot covers the keyhole) and a device for counting the number of times the door is opened. The lock is inscribed, 'If I had ye gift of tongue, I would declare and do no wrong, who ye are ye come by stealth, to impare my master's wealth.' Clearly, Lord Bristol distrusted his lady. Among the pictures in the house, which also contains some excellent china and furniture, is the famous painting attributed to Marc Gheeraerdts of Queen Elizabeth on a litter carried by members of her court.

Raleigh had laid out gardens of some elaboration, which were flooded in the eighteenth century when Capability Brown dammed the Yeo to make the lake in his extremely attractive parkland, now finely wooded and populated with deer. Just by a little bridge under the mound of the old castle is a stone seat said (among others, unfortunately) to be the one in which Raleigh was sitting smoking a pipe when his surprised servant drenched him in water to extinguish the fire. Another seat across the stream was a favourite with Alexander Pope, who was a visitor here. In the old dairy, adjoining the house, a Roman pavement found in 1836 at Lenthay Green, a rough but vigorous picture of Apollo and Marsyas, has been reset in the floor.

Eastward, past the park, the A 30 cuts through the Somerset town of Milborne Port to reach Purse Caundle, where the grey stone manor dating from the fifteenth century is frequently open to the public. The estate belonged in the thirteenth century to a certain John Aleyn, who held it direct from the King by Serjeanty, his duties being 'to keep or lodge the King's sick or injured hounds at the King's cost when the King hunts game in Blakemore'. He was also allowed one penny a year for keeping up the park fences of Gillingham. Of course, King John is supposed to have been here, and his hounds, legend says, can be heard on the bowling green on both Christmas and Midsummer Eve. The present building was probably begun by the son of a Richard Long, who bought the estate in 1429. The hall range dates from the time of Edward IV, the hall itself having a splendid arch-braced collar-beam roof, with tie-beams and king-posts added later, probably because the roof was pushing the walls out. A dainty oriel at the eastern end of the solar has looked delicately on to the village street for five centuries, and additions to the house were built during Tudor and Stuart times.

The village church, not far off, has much atmosphere despite Victorian restoration. The chantry chapel, entered through a fifteenth-century screen, has some excellent small brasses, while fragments of medieval glass can be found in some of the windows. The son of a seventeenth-century rector, Nicholas Highmore (1614-85), was a physician who practised at Sherborne, a friend of William Harvey, and a famous anatomist. A portion of the skull is still called the Antrum of Highmore. Another native of Purse Caundle, Peter Mews, fought for the King in the Civil War, suffered 30 wounds in his service, and was taken prisoner at Naseby. Having fled to Holland and served in Flanders under the Duke of York, he went to Oxford after the Restoration and became president of St. John's College. In 1684 he was bishop of Winchester, an office which did not inhibit him from taking the field again at the head of his own troop and getting yet another wound at Sedgmoor.

At Stourton Caundle, two miles away, the fifteenth-century church has an air of antiquity (but not neglect) and a pulpit also of the fifteenth century. South of the Blandford road, Holwell, isolated on a cul-de-sac, is a small group of eighteenth-century cottages with the vicarage and the church, which has outside some satisfyingly grotesque gargoyles and inside excellent roofs and a west-country type Perpendicular arcade with scrolls and demi-angels round the capitals.

Holnest, on the road from Dorchester to Sherborne is simply a church in a field. That the church is of the fourteenth century with box pews and a seventeenth-century pulpit makes it worth a visit. At Long Burton, an otherwise dull village, the church is also of some interest. In a little seventeenth-century chapel north of the chancel are two elaborate canopied altar tombs, both in the same style. Each bears a male and a female effigy, the man in armour. The eastern tomb is that of Sir John Fitzjames of Leweston and his wife, a sister of Sir George Trenchard of Wolfeton. 'A smooth knave as any liveth and a false', was Raleigh's description of Sir John, but of course that does not appear on his tomb, and anyway Fitzjames had the manors of Longburton and Holnest, which Raleigh coveted. In the recess below the effigies are sculpted bones, skulls, and spade. The other monument is to Sir Henry Winston, of Standish, Gloucestershire, and his wife Eleanor, and the effigy of a man in armour below them is that of Sir Henry's father, Thomas. The Fitzjames tomb was erected by Leweston Fitzjames, the Winston tomb by the lady he married, the daughter of Sir Henry Winston. The painted inscription on the wall behind tells how she 'beinge denyed to repayre and erect these remembrances of her parents in the church of Standish, where they lie buried, hath transferred them thence and placed them here, where a part of their posteritie is now by the mercifull providence of the Almightie planted'. Over the south door the arms of Charles II (in much need of restoring) are set in a frame with two Biblical quotations expressive of Royalist sentiment after the Commonwealth—'Curse not the king, noe, not in thy thought', and 'Fear thou the Lord and the King and meddle not with them that are given to change'.

Folke, almost due east, on a cul-de-sac, has a stone seventeenth-century manor house, the home of the Chafins before they moved to Chettle. It stands opposite the church, which dates from 1628, and retains many of its original fittings, including bench ends and oak screen.

North of the main road from Sherborne to Yeovil the countryside undulates gently, giving a warm, intimate landscape green with wood and lush pasture. The villages are all gold and remote and as yet unspoiled by the advance of Yeovil, which is physically close but separated by the cleft made in the hills of inferior oolite by the River Yeo, which forms the county boundary. Nether Compton is the first village, round a green, reached by a narrow, winding road, and furnished with a thirteenth-century church and an inn, the Griffin's Head, of 1599. Over Compton is no more than a handful of cottages in the grounds of Compton House (rebuilt in the nineteenth century) in front of which, shaded by a huge and flamboyant cedar tree is the little wagon-roofed church. This contains a two-tiered Jacobean pulpit and in the north chapel an agglomeration of monuments to various members of the Goodden family. One of these is worth finding Over Compton for. It is a superb full-length portrait sculpture of an elderly gentleman who died in 1828. He is portly, he stoops a little, and leans on a stick. He wears a double-breasted coat with tails, breeches, and gaiters. His clothes are creased, and there is some pull on the coat buttons. This, with the crinkles at the elbows and under the left shoulder, the sagging of the breeches, the supporting of the body's weight on the stick, the set of the elderly head in the deep collar, the furrows in the brow echoed by the upward sweep of the thin hair, make a vivid and powerful likeness of an old man, careless of his appearance, a little irascible, and perhaps tired of life. The artist may have been Flaxman.

Trent, a mile north, is a most unusually scattered village, with an equally unusual number of old buildings of some size and importance. The church has a medieval spire, rebuilt in 1925, and an interior full of interest. The intricately carved oak chancel screen and rood loft, dating from the fifteenth century, with seventeenth-century alterations, is said to have come from Glastonbury. The sixteenth-century bench ends are elaborately carved with symbols of the Passion and with other devices, and four of them together make the prayer, '*Ave Maria Gratia Plena Domi-*

nus Tecum Amen'. The hideous pulpit is Dutch, dating from about 1600. Two fourteenth-century effigies, one of a knight, one a civilian in a gown but wearing a sword, lie in the north chapel, and the soffit of the arch leading into the chancel has a painted inscription whose letters are alternate ways up, so that it is difficult to decipher impartially from one side or the other. On the edge of the churchyard, which contains a slender cross, stands an early sixteenth-century house called The Chantry, with conspicuous old stone chimneys. Possibly it was built for a priest. The Manor house, north of the church incorporates some medieval building, though much of it dates from the seventeenth and eighteenth centuries. It sheltered Charles II during his flight to the coast after Worcester.

Until 70 years ago Trent was part of Somerset, like Sandford Orcas, which lies in a pretty valley among tumbled little hills on the edge of the county north from Sherborne. The second part of the name comes from the Norman lords of the manor, called de Orescuiltz, to whom it belonged for three generations. In course of time it descended to Edward Knoyle, who probably built the manor house sometime after 1533, and seems to have employed the mason who worked on the west wing at Athelhampton, for the similarities between the decorative details there and on the porch at Sandford Orcas are quite striking. Since a Knoyle, possibly Edward's son, was married to Catherine, the sister of Nicholas Martyn, the Athelhampton connection is probable enough. The house, standing higher than the road and approached through a stone gatehouse, contains much sixteenth- and seventeenth-century woodwork. The weathered stone of the church exterior, just by the manor, overlooking a sparkling little stream, is more pleasing than the over-restored interior which has, however, a fifteenth-century screen at the west end, and in the south chapel a wall monument to William Knoyle (who died in 1608) with figures of himself and two wives, the first with four swaddled children who died in infancy, and the second with three sons and four daughters who survived. Poyntington, on a crossroad with a signpost plumb in the middle, is much restored (this applies to both church and manor) but charming. Where the road through Oborne joins the A 30 east of Sherborne is the little sixteenth-century Chapel of St. Cuthbert, in fact the chancel of the old parish church, formerly a chapel of ease to Sherborne, the rest of which was destroyed in the nineteenth century when the new church was built. Its bare and austere interior accommodates a seventeenth-century oak pulpit, as white as the pews in Winterborne Tomson, and some simple wood furniture, as well as a number of fourteenth- or fifteenth-century tiles cemented into panels and leaning against the wall. It is used as a church every Trinity Sunday.

South-west of Sherborne, in Bradford Abbas, a dull village otherwise, a gem of a church, mainly fifteenth century, has a tower with carvings (we are on the Somerset border), a richly ornamented porch, a panelled roof with painted angels, a particularly good set of carved bench ends, and among other features some fierce gargoyles on the north aisle. Not far off at Wyke, a moated Jacobean house, originally a grange of Sherborne Abbey, stands at the end of a cul-de-sac. The railway and the smallest station imaginable separate it from a farm with two long, narrow, sixteenth-century barns in one continuous range, with a collar-beam roof. In the other direction, on the left bank of the Yeo west of Bradford Abbas is the surviving part of the seat of the Horsey family, Clifton Maybank. It is visible from the road, half hidden in trees, and less than half the house it was. It came to the Horseys in the early fifteenth century by marriage with an heiress of the Maubanks, and by judicious purchases and marriages the family had become owners of an enormous estate by 1564. Eighty years later, Sir George Horsey died in a debtor's prison. Of the house only a wing remains *in situ* now, but pieces of it are to be found in several places. In 1786 Edward Phelips of Montacute bought the front and porch which he added to the west front at Montacute to form what is now known as the Clifton Maybank corridor. In 1800 the Jacobean gatehouse went to Hinton St. George, also in Somerset. A heraldic finial survives at Compton House, Over Compton, and some stonework was used to make a gateway in the Manor House, Beaminster. Other parts are said to be at Brympton d'Evercy.

Accessible from here through Beer Hackett, Lillington lies towards the southern edge of the limestone ridge on which Sherborne itself stands, a remote and peaceful hamlet at the end of a road. The church is built on a sort of platform on the side of a gentle slope, reaching out into the valley, and has a neat, clean, bright but somewhat featureless interior. Next to it the sixteenth-century barn has an arch-braced collar-beam roof.

The golden-stone village of Yetminster, approached from the north by a small, humpy, sixteenth-century bridge, has many houses with mullioned and dripstoned windows, and doorways with four-centred heads. The fifteenth-century church, light, but over-restored, has some good brasses of the Horsey family. At Ryme Intrinseca, which has less character than its name suggests, the church, approached by an avenue of carefully clipped yews, is partly seventeenth century. On the north wall of the chancel an inscription to a vicar who died in 1664 reads:

> *Reader, weep on his herse*
> *in whom did dwell all vertu*
> *es yet twas love made*
> *him excell.*

To the south-west, Chetnole straggles along the river Wriggle, and the next village, Leigh, has similarly no pretensions to shape. In a field near Leigh is the remains of a miz-maze. All that can be seen is a hexagonal enclosure about 20 yards across, with a very low hump in the middle, a bank about a foot high and a slight trace of a ditch. As late as 1800 it is said to have had banks in an intricate pattern, but was allowed to deteriorate after the enclosure in that year of the land it stood on. An annual repair used formerly to take place, with festivities, possibly for May Day, but tradition associates it with witches, who are said to have used it as a gathering place. The last witch to be burned in England (she was executed in Maumbury Rings in the late seventeenth century) is supposed to have been arrested while at a meeting here.

South of Chetnole and Leigh, Blackmore Vale runs down to the foot of the great chalk hills between the main roads from Dorchester to Yeovil and Sherborne. Westward, under steep and wooded Bubb Down Hill, at the end of an old road, a long, banked and hedged cul-de-sac, lies Melbury Bubb. The church is remarkable for its pre-Conquest font, the base of a cross hollowed out to form a bowl, and most intricately carved. It is incomprehensible until one realises it is upside down. There are also fragments of fifteenth-century glass, including two in a nave window representing the Annunciation, and a figure of Christ showing the five wounds.

Under High Stoy lies the church at Hilfield, another which has lost its village. This simple little flint and rubble building has a set of bench ends whose date is disputed, some thinking them medieval, some dating them from the nineteenth century. No matter. They are finely carved with scenes from the New Testament, and like so many small things in this county of contrarieties worth making a journey to see. That they stand in an isolated, minute church, on the lower slopes of the soaring escarpment between the clay and the chalk, the Vale and the Downs, seems altogether appropriate.

The sharp contrast exemplified here becomes the more remarkable when one compares Hilfield and its surroundings with the suave suburbanity of Branksome Park, the forbidding heath behind the mud flats of Arne and the southern shore of Poole Harbour, the cruel cliffscape of Purbeck and Portland, and the black rocks of the west Dorset coast, so rich in treasure for the palaeontologist. Bearing in mind not only all this, but—to name just a few features of many—the sophistication of modern industry at Poole, the artificial elegance of Milton Abbas, and the relics of more barbaric times and attitudes at Corfe Castle, the old hill forts, and other prehistoric sites, one may legitimately marvel at the variety to be found in this small and still largely unspoiled county. Anyone who wants a visual summary of England outside the mountains and the industrial conurbations may safely be brought to Dorset, and having toured it be left to meditate at Hilfield beside High Stoy.

Bibliography

BAYLEY, A. R., *The Great Civil War in Dorset*, 1910

BICKLEY, F., *Where Dorset meets Devon*, 1911

CLEGG, A. L., *History of Wimborne Minster and District*, 1960

DAVIES, G. M., *The Dorset Coast, A Geological Guide*, 2nd edition, 1956

FOWLER, P. J., *Wessex* (Regional Archaeologies), 1967

GRIGSON, G., Introduction to *Selected Poems of William Barnes*, 1950

GRINSELL, L. V., *The Archaeology of Wessex*, 1958

HARDY, F. E., *The Life of Thomas Hardy*, 1962

HEATH, F. R., *Dorset* (The Little Guides), revised by E. T. Long, 1949

HUTCHINS, J., *History and Antiquities of the County of Dorset*, 3rd edition, corrected, augmented, and improved by W. Shipp and J. W. Hodson, 1861-73

LLOYD, R., *Dorset Elizabethans At Home and Abroad*, 1967

OSWALD, A., *Country Houses of Dorset*, 2nd edition, 1959

PITT RIVERS, M., *Dorset, A Shell Guide*, 1966

ROBINSON, C. E., *A Royal Warren, or Picturesque Rambles in the Isle of Purbeck*, 1882

Royal Commission on Historical Monuments, England, *An Inventory of the Historical Monuments in Dorset, Vol. 1, West*, 1952

SMITH, H. P., *History of the Town & County of the Borough of Poole*, 1948-51

TREVES, SIR F., *Highways and Byways in Dorset*, 1906

UDAL, J. S., *Dorsetshire Folklore*, with a foresay by the late William Barnes, D.D., 1922

WEINSTOCK, M. B., *Old Dorset*, 1967

WIGHTMAN, R., *Portrait of Dorset*, 1965

WILDMAN, W. B., *Short History of Sherborne*, 1902

Articles in the following periodicals have been of value:—
  Proceedings of the Dorset Natural History and Archaeological Society
  Somerset and Dorset Notes and Queries
  Dorset Year Book
  Dorset
  Country Life (for articles by A. Oswald)
  Antiquity

This is an exhaustive list neither of printed sources in general nor even of the works I have occasionally consulted in writing this book, but only of these to which my debt is significant. I have also omitted the numerous leaflets and booklets, guides to churches and country houses, which I have found invaluable. It would be wrong not to record here my gratitude for the help I have had at need from the staff of the Public Reference Libraries in both Bournemouth and Poole.

Index

The numerals in **bold** type refer to the figure numbers of the illustrations

Index

Index

Index

Index

Index